Ethics and the Wars of Insurgency

Ethics and the Wars of Insurgency

Somalia to Syria

KENNETH L. VAUX

WIPF & STOCK · Eugene, Oregon

ETHICS AND THE WARS OF INSURGENCY
Somalia to Syria

Copyright © 2014 Kenneth L. Vaux. All rights reserved. Except for brief quotations in critical publications or reviews, no part of this book may be reproduced in any manner without prior written permission from the publisher. Write: Permissions, Wipf and Stock Publishers, 199 W. 8th Ave., Suite 3, Eugene, OR 97401.

Where indicated, Scripture quotations are take from the Holy Bible, New International Version®, NIV® Copyright © 1973, 1978, 1984, 2011 by Biblica, Inc.™ Used by permission. All rights reserved worldwide.

Wipf & Stock
An imprint of Wipf and Stock Publishers
199 W. 8th Ave., Suite 3
Eugene, OR 97401

www.wipfandstock.com

isbn 13: 978-1-62564-183-0

Manufactured in the U.S.A.

Many thanks to Nathan Rhoads, Ian Creeger, and my long-time editor at the Press, Christian Amondson, for exacting and caring partnership.

Christmastide 2013. Eastertide 2014. Cold and warm.
War and Peace. Darkness and light.

Contents

Introduction | ix

1 The Heritage and Destiny of the Somalian People: Etiology and Eschatology as Ethical Norms | 1

2 Nationhood and Anthropogenic Famine: How History and Biology Have Shaped the Somali Crisis | 11

3 Ecology and Economy: Apocalypse and Hunger | 23

4 Just War and International Law: Axiology and the Search for a New Morality of the Common Good | 31

5 Ethnic Eviction: Fratricide And Genocide: Anthropology, Psychology and Violence | 45

6 Theology, Polity, and the Pacific Vision: Futuristic Hope, Pastoral Restoration, and the Glimpse of a New World Order of Human Rights and Fulfillment | 55

Addendum: American Led Attack on Syria? (September 2013) | 137

Introduction

AMAR HAMMAMI, RAISED IN Daphne, Alabama, is being tracked down with orders to kill—by two parties, each resolute that he must be eliminated. The American CIA and the broader movement of anti-terrorist operatives of the US government as well as Al Shabab operatives in Somalia are on his tail with their national and international spying networks.

An honor student, president of his high school class, son of a liberal Muslim dad and a Southern Baptist mom, he began to change when he was sixteen, becoming an intense Islamic believer and activist, eventually leaving his Alabama home for Toronto, Egypt, and eventually Somalia. Others of his ilk would end up in Afghanistan. He had become a true believer.

One of the top terrorist suspects in the US, he is charged with a "religious killing" that took twenty lives, including another American—Shirwa Ahmed, from Minneapolis—who had achieved the dubious reputation as the first American suicide bomber.

Along the way he has managed to offend his compatriots in the Shabab "youth corps" causing them, as we would say in Chicago, to put out a "contract"—calling him to turn himself in within fifteen days or face killing. If his ragged Somalian corps doesn't get him first we can trust that the US "security web" will carry out a "designated killing" or "drone attack." He is damned and dead in one scenario or the other. In a comment on PBS Evening News (February 8, 2013), Mark Shields, an astute political commentator, remarked that drones and non-legal killings of Americans

Introduction

and others in other countries is not only unacknowledged and is considered non-discussable—it is "the unquestioned new religion of this city" (Washington, DC).

Hammami's case points to the theological undercurrents of the "War on Terrorism"—that epic conflagration with its epicenter in the Israeli/Palestinian conflict—a national (US) and international "war unto death" which has roots in the appearance of the three faiths of Abraham—a fateful trifurcation (see my *Jew, Christian, Muslim*) which now pits Jewish and Christian fundamentalist ideologues and " freedom fighters" on the one hand against the "Jihadist" or "Islamist" ideologues and "freedom fighters " on the other. Execution of these offensive and defensive endeavors—which are as old as the Constantinian and Crusading impulses of Christianity and the Muslim conquests—today consumes an alarming percentage of the national expenditures of Israel, America and the "West," and the Muslim world from its realms. All these commitments—for military, security, and espionage hegemony—not only fail to bring security but threaten the peace and justice of global humanity along with the well-being of the world itself.

Toward the end of my book on the Gulf War I wrote of "Another Vision of Peace":

> The world of nuclear weapons stockpiling, the arms race, and belligerent diplomacy is not the peaceable kingdom envisioned by Isaiah in his prophesies or Henri Rousseau in his painting, a world in which swords (or rifle butts) are beaten into plowshares and "they will study and learn war no more" (Isaiah 2:4). The news on BBC carried a fascinating picture. A US soldier~ assisted by several Kurds was pushing around large stones with his rifle butt and together they formed them into a large circle near Zakho. They were outlining areas for toilets and cooking, tents and recreation areas for the protective encampments being set up by the Allies which they hoped would lure the fleeting and dying Kurds down from the mountains of the Turkish border. The image of

Introduction

a rifle butt being beaten into a plowshare was moving. One was led to wonder why we do not employ all of the armies of the world in such peace-building and peace-keeping missions.[1]

In this violent century we have "beaten our plowshares into swords" as the nations of the world have transfigured their national budgets from humanitarian to armamentarian purposes. Now, in this millennial moment, we seem to have arrived at a messianic reversal, a season when we will "study war no more." Is such a new day at last possible and feasible? Some glimpses of hope rise on the horizon as Western nations at least speak of a "peace dividend."

In Advent of 1990, when the war broke out in the Persian Gulf, I was resident of Christ Church College in Oxford, on sabbatical from the University of Illinois in Chicago. Then I organized ethical reflection on that war around the War Requiems, including that of Benjamin Britten and the powerful WWI poetry of Wilfred Owen. This sequel reflection, begun in Advent 1992, on Operation Restore Hope in Somalia is organized around Randall Thompson's "sequence of sacred choruses," *The Peaceable Kingdom*, based on texts from the Book of Isaiah and on Edward Hicks' painting *The Peaceable Kingdom*. Owen's poems speak poignantly of the agony of war-making. Thompson's choruses speak proleptically of the ecstasy of peace-making. Advent and Lent, with their apocalyptic and eschatological mood—seasons when we ponder transcending dimensions of natural and historical events—provide the backdrop of meaning for such global historical events.

The Somalia incursion invites spiritual and ethical interpretation even more than did the Gulf War. The Gulf War elicited religious rhetoric from all participants but it was at root a matter of geopolitical prestige and economic hegemony. It boiled down to oil. As then Secretary of State Baker American said, "If Kuwait's main export commodity was oranges [or Somalia's provocative incense] nothing would have happened."

---

1. Kenneth L. Vaux, *Ethics and the Gulf War: Religion, Rhetoric, and Righteousness* (Boulder, CO: Westview, 1992), 155.

Introduction

Now again, Western nations, steeped in Judeo-Christian meanings and moralities, venture into an imperiled and impoverished Islamic land. The purity of this tribal Muslim land—in their own subliminal piety—had already been twice violated: by the degradation of starvation and death and by the presence of the Gentile. Unlike the sanction-induced hunger in Iraq, in Somalia then in Iran and Afghanistan deprivation and starvation continues—by human contrivance—to ride like an apocalyptic horseman. We saw again that strange admixture of purity and poverty, so typical of societies around the world where Islam has exhibited its tropism toward the poor, in an event on December 14, 1992.

The vehicle was driven by French soldiers. It stopped and out stepped an attractive young Somalian woman. Assuming that she had consorted with the pagan foreigners, in a scene reminiscent of Jesus and the woman caught in adultery, she was stripped, beaten, and stoned. Graciously, a Zorba-like Christ appeared with a long knife and held back the zealous youths until the woman was safe.

Unlike the Gulf War, where the purpose was to repel aggression and protect vital interests, this incursion was intended to rescue and heal, not humiliate and destroy. It has recently come to light that a purpose secondary to the primary goal of Operation Desert Storm—to expel Saddam Hussein from Kuwait—was to demolish the infrastructure: the water- and food-delivery system, the sanitation, communication, and healthcare systems. Because of these objectives, though certainly not our nation's intention, Western action did, in fact, increase disease, impoverishment, and death in this poor, far-distant land.

In Somali, perhaps because of some residual, even subconscious guilt about that incursion, we now sought to edify, to establish infrastructure, open food lines, and reconstitute a decimated people. If the parades and enthusiastic self-adulation which followed Desert Storm were in part understandable as a rectification of disgrace of Vietnam, where our tattered boys returned home to disdain and disregard, this venture into Somalia might well serve to rectify the subconscious guilt for the massive inhumanity inflicted on the Iraqi people in Desert Storm. Even though that

Introduction

violence was extended in retaliation against another inhumanity perpetrated by Saddam Hussein, not only on the people of Kuwait but on the Shia and Kurds in Iraq proper, in our own collective conscience a residue of guilt endured over the killing of children, the severance of life lines of food and medical sustenance, and the final massacre.

The connections of meaning between the events of Vietnam, Iraq, and Somalia, perhaps even the oblique cross-references to Bosnia and Palestine (deported refugees), are suggestive as we decipher this development. So are the larger ligatures linking the Crusades of the Middle Ages, colonialism in the nineteenth century, and the Cold War of the twentieth. The realm of Spirit and ethics must be consulted to search out the meaning of this history. Such hermeneutical purpose ponders the turgor of such ligatures (*religare*/religion).

The purpose of this book, as in my study of the Gulf War earlier in that decade, is to try to see a big picture or meaning within the flow of concrete events. In the unfolding drama of nature and history, what my teachers Helmut Thielicke and Carl Friedrich Von Weizsacker might call *Heilesgeschichte* (a Holy Story), we ask: what does it mean that 1992 ended with the words Somalia and Bosnia on the lips of winter holiday celebrants around the world? Here is the thesis I will put before the reader and attempt to interpret:

> Through the justice of God expressed in time and space, an eschatological (here, yet still there [unfinished]) kingdom of peace is being anticipated and partially actualized as the worlds of affluent prosperity and abject poverty meet in Somalia in the aborted campaign called Operation Restore Hope.
>
> Drawing texts from Isaiah, Randall Thompson portrays a drama unfolding in the world, a drama of sin and guilt, judgment and new possibility, sacrifice and redemption. These epiphenomena portray the ethical significance of historical events such as the crisis in Somalia. The drama of life, which in the biblical tradition is the stuff of ethics, moves through the stages of

Introduction

memory, presence, and hope as the human community is confronted with divine presence as this is delivered and received as judgment and grace. These are not strictly temporal categories, but spatial-temporal. In biblical science, apocalyptic is the surprise spontaneity of nature just as eschatology is the surprise implicit in time.

The apocalyptic is to space what the eschatological is to time. Natural and historical drama has a story line plus flash-backs and flash-forwards. Ethics is a historical and natural inquiry transformed by these transcending dimensions. Ethics is the observation of what is in light of what ought to be or what could be. Ethics seeks to explain (lay out) the meaning of events.

The global ethical crisis we signify by Somalia also falls into dimensions of past, present, and future. Individuals and nations receive judgment in terms of what they have been, who they presently are, and what they will be. The thesis I explore in this book is that events in Somalia, with cognate events in Yugoslavia, Russia, Sudan, India, and Palestine, are portentous in that they signal an agonal judgment on past wrongs and anticipations of a new peace. I will develop this thesis in six stages. Borrowing six leitmotifs from Randall Thompson's rendition of the Isaiah passages, we will identify normative themes which in turn apply interpretatively to the Somalia saga:

I. "Ye shall have a song, as in the night when a holy solemnity is kept; and gladness of heart, as when one goeth with a pipe, to come into the mountain of the LORD" (Isa 30:29).[2]

  Themes: Etiology: the pastoral heritage of Somalia
  Eschatology: the post–ColdWar destiny of the people

II. "The noise of a multitude in the mountains, like as of a great people; a tumultuous noise of the kingdoms of nations gathered together: the LORD of hosts mustereth the host of the battle. They come from a far country, from the end of heaven, even the LORD, and the weapons of his indignation, to

2. Unless otherwise noted, Scripture quotations are taken from the KJV.

Introduction

destroy the whole land. / Their bows also shall dash the young men to pieces; and they shall have no pity on the fruit of the womb; their eye shall not spare children. / Every one that is found shall be thrust through; and every one that is joined unto them shall fall by the sword. Their children also shall be dashed to pieces before their eyes; their houses shall be spoiled, and their wives ravished. / Therefore shall all hands be faint, and every man's heart shall melt. And they shall be afraid: pangs and sorrow shall take hold of them; they shall be in pain as a woman that travaileth: they shall be amazed at one another; their faces shall be as flames" (Isa 13:4–5, 18, 15–16, 7–8).

    Themes: History: nationhood, international politics, law
                  Biology: anthropogenic famine and the slaughter of innocents

III. "The Paper reeds by the brooks, by the mouth of the brooks, and everything sown by the brooks, shall wither, be driven away, and be no more" (Isa 19:7).

    Themes: Ecology: drought, desertification, and a fragile ecostructure
                  Economy: dependence, independence, and interdependence

IV. "Say ye to the righteous, that it shall be well with him: for they shall eat the fruit of their doings. Woe unto the wicked! it shall be ill with him: for the reward of his hands shall be given him (Isa 3:10–11).

"Woe unto them that join house to house, that lay field to field, till there be no place, that they may be placed alone in the midst of the earth!" (Isa 5:8).

    Themes: Axiology: the covenants of life with life—Noachic, Abrahamic, Mosaic, Levitic, Davidic, Christic

V. "Have ye not known? Have ye not heard? Hath it not been told to you from the beginning? Have ye not understood from the foundations of the earth?" (Isa 40:21)

Introduction

    Themes: Anthropology: racism, genocide

VI. "For ye shall go out with joy, and be led forth in peace: the mountains and the hills shall break forth before you into singing, and all the trees of the fields shall clap their hands" (Isa 55:12).

    Themes: Theology: the futuristic hope for pastoral restoration

               Polity: a new world order, subsequent human rights, peace on earth

Somalia, December 1992. "Soldiers did not expect so many lush fields, boys with rifles and, sometimes crowds of healthy people."[3] Verdant fields and violent fledglings—the dying and the living. Understanding the spectacle of good and evil in their deeper meaning requires vision *sub specie aeternitatis*.

The normative motifs of etiology and eschatology, history and biology, ecology and economy, axiology and anthropology, theology and polity provide windows into the significance of remarkable events. Such portentous events are observed when the world's warriors converge to make peace and those trained to kill to secure the living now arrive to bring life to save the dying.

EXCURSUS: WILL RENO, FEARLESS VAGABOND AND TROUBLESHOOTER IN SOMALIA, POLITICAL SCIENTIST, AND SCHOLAR-TEACHER EXTRAORDINAIRE

His Canadian ancestors, it is reported, were supposed to be among the victims of the Battle of Bull Run and Custer's "Last Stand" in the Dakotas. They escaped, shall we say, by the skin of their scalp. Now their cunning and bravery lives on in their descendent—Will Reno.

    At present he is skiing across Newfoundland, trekking across Somalia, or most probably—right now—sand-skiing across

---

3. *New York Times*, December 27, 1992, E6.

Introduction

Afghanistan. In his muscle-beach T-shirt he goes into Mogadishu fearlessly, known by everyone—Catholic sister, teenage child soldier, tribal elder. He won't be kidnapped, and if he were by mistake he would be delivered immediately to the leaders with the words, "It's Will—deliver him safely."

He loves the place—godforsaken by the world. He finds it a most beautiful place with endearing people.

1

The Heritage and Destiny of the Somalian People
Etiology and Eschatology as Ethical Norms

Ye shall have a song as in the night when a holy solemnity is kept . . .
(Isa 30:29)

BORDERED BY THE INDIAN Ocean on the east, the Gulf of Aden and the delta of the Red Sea on the north, and Ethiopia and Kenya on the west and south, Somalia juts out as a Rhino's horn, a protrusion of East Central Africa that fits snugly into the southern edge of Arabia, now Yemen, before the plate-tectonic shift. Ruled colonially by Italy and Great Britain, Somalia received its independence in 1960. The exuberance of independence was quickly dampened by the Cold War, in which both Russia and the West exploited the beauteous, wise, and poetic ancient land for geopolitical purpose. Its population of some eight million has now probably been decimated twice or three times by famine and fratricide. Now with the massive starvation of the population under five years of age, it has

Ethics and the Wars of Insurgency

become questionable whether a viable new generation will arise to inherit this good earth.

Constituted by two ethnic communities, the Sab have engaged in sedentary agriculture and the Somali in nomadic herding. In the brutal infighting that followed the deportation of General Siad Barre in 1989, both fields and flocks were left destitute. Centuries of tribal conflict have been exacerbated by disruption caused by colonialism and the Cold War. The Italian protectorate, which began in 1885, was united with the post-WWI British trusteeship in the northwest in 1950. In 1960 Britain granted independence to its nineteenth-century protectorate and in that same summer it joined with the Italian jurisdiction to form the independent Somali Republic. As has so often been the case in Africa, freedom often led to turbulence and chaos.

During the colonial period, various parties vied for the limited influence that occupation might allow: SYL (the Somalia Youth League), USP (United Somali Party), and SNL (Somali National League) retained some heritage of the traditional tribal authority. After independence, a fragile coalition of these parties sought to govern. Two weak administrations served throughout the 1960s as Cold War gerrymandering mounted.

On October 21, 1969, a Supreme Revolutionary Council seized power after the president was assassinated and the assembly was dissolved. A severe drought in 1975 killed tens of thousands as nature herself added apocalypse to societal antagonisms. Who can forget the moving scene on CBS Evening News (December 8, 1992) when correspondent Dan Rather visited Baidoa before the Marines arrived. In a makeshift hospital he was asked to hold down and comfort a small child who was writhing in pain after the side of his head had been shot off by the violent gunmen. "This is apocalypse now!" Rather cried through his tears.

In the late 1970s, aided by Soviet and Cuban forces, Ethiopian rebels defeated Somali forces in Ethiopia and forced as many as two million Somalian-Ethiopian refugees across the border. Guerilla raids across this border continued until a peace agreement was reached in 1988. Beginning in the early 1980s, General

The Heritage and Destiny of the Somalian People

Barre's government began what can only be described as a rage and quasi-genocidal war against the three major clans: the Isaac, Ogaden, and Hawiye—ostensibly because of their support of three anti-government parties: SNM (Somali National Movement), SPM (Somali Patriotic Movement), and UMC (United Somali Congress). The Geneva Conventions and all rules of "just war" had been violated as the government (as in Iraq and Syria) had looted, raped, and killed its own people.[1] By late 1988 tens of thousands had been killed and, like numbers of refugees, had fled to Ethiopia. In 1992 clan leaders and gunmen-riding technicals were forced to desist. In their looting of food and medicines from the NGOs (non-governmental organizations), many fled into hiding across the Ethiopian border.

After Mohammed Siad Barre became ruler in 1974, Somalia became the first black African state to sign a friendship treaty with the Soviet Union. After Soviet favor was redirected toward Ethiopia with the leftist military coup against Haile Selassie, Presidents Carter and Regan cozied up to Somalia in order to maintain access to the Soviet naval and air base at Berbera on the Indian Ocean coast.

In the early 1990s, when the Soviet Union collapsed and its hegemony diminished, a political vacuum ensued. The corruptions of ancient tribal antagonisms erupted again to the surface. Like Indo-European raiders to the northwest, these people had a long heritage of raiding, animal seizing, capture of women, and deportation of children. These vicious archaic patterns always threatened the dominant pastoral establishment of farming and nomadic herd-keeping.

The wealthy and powerful Western nations had to intervene. The twin devastations of famine and civil war had already killed half a million persons, and humanitarian appeal to the heart along with strategic appeal to the head convinced the US to reassert its interest in the region. With the demise of the Soviet Union and the end of the Cold War, the strategic concern to protect the Saudi oil

---

1. Human Rights Watch, *Somalia: A Government at War with Its Own People*, Africa Watch Report (New York: Human Rights Watch, 1990), 2

Ethics and the Wars of Insurgency

fields, the assets of its allies in the Arabian Gulf, and the concern over access to the Red Sea had diminished as focus now centered on an unconscionable human-made famine and its consequence of mass starvation for the innocent. The issue had now taken on ethical, moral, and theological—even biblical—dimensions—thus this study.

THE PASTORAL HERITAGE

From Sir Richard Burton's first description of the proud and majestic peoples of northern Somalia,[2] we have known these herders of camels, sheep, goats, and ponies as strongly independent people bound fiercely by kinship ties. In the barren pastoral landscape lineage, identity, and destiny are linked to one's ancestral genealogy. Assertion of rights, feuding, demands for honor, and abrogations of power have led some observers to find in this society an "omnipresence of struggle." Of the six major clans four are primarily northern pastoral nomads—the Dir Isaaq, Hawiye and Daa Rood. Two former clans—the Digil and Rahanween—are more active in the south. Most Somalis are either centrally or peripherally attached to these clan structures, at least offering tribute as dues-payers. Recorded history first speaks of these clans in the thirteenth century.[3]

Zeila in the north and Mogadishu in the south were port trading centers founded by Arab and Persian immigrants early in the tenth century. The earliest inculturation therefore is Hamitic in race and language and Islamic in belief and ethics. By the seventeenth century the Sharifs of Mukha and the Imaams of Oman had established Islamic orthodoxy and orthopraxy in the north and south. To this day it must be acknowledged that the penetration of

2. Richard F. Burton, *First Footsteps in East Africa; or, An Exploration of Harar* (London: Longman, Brown, Green, and Longmans, 1856).

3. M. Andrzejewski, "Military Organization and Society" (1954), quoted in I. M. Lewis, *A Pastoral Democracy: A Study of Pastoralism and Politics among the Northern Somali of the Horn of Africa* (London: Oxford University Press, 1967), 247.

The Heritage and Destiny of the Somalian People

Islamic vision and persuasion has always been attenuated in this unique culture. No further colonization or missionizing occurred until the nineteenth century, when Egypt conceded its influence over Ethiopia and Somalia to France and Britain. Brief interludes of dependency to India and Italy punctuated this legacy. While the colonial incursions and later Cold War machinations did much to destroy the heritage and inherent fabric of Somalia, and while sizable Somali populations live today in Jibuti, Ethiopia, and Kenya, it remained a nation of organic legacy and structure rather than a contrived multinational entity, such as its neighbor Ethiopia. Somalia is a nation in the sense of Luke's designation in the Acts of the Apostles:

> He made from one blood every nation of men to live on all the face of the earth, having determined allotted periods and the boundaries of their habitation. (17:26, paraphrase)

The legacy of the Cold War was to turn the natural tribal rivalry of these people into fratricide and suicide. Predatorial violence turned in on its own people. Like inner-city violence in American cities, blacks turned on blacks in drug trafficking, looting, and gang violence. Deprived of contributing occupation, young people took up guns and turned against their own. Like persons with Lesch-Nyan disease, anorexia, or "silence of the lambs," persons devoured their own flesh. Like Saddam Hussein, Said Barre eventually resorted in masochistic rage to torching his own people and scorching his own home.

The pastoral heritage of the Somali people makes this recent violation and aberration of international order and justice all the more tragic. Firm in their belief that pasturage and all the bounty of the earth is the gift of God and therefore is adequately provident for the sustenance of families and societies, now the land and peoples found themselves in the grip of animosity, rivalry, and brutal antagonism. Now apocalyptic vistas of parched and famished landscape displaced the verdant and provident gardens.

Ethics and the Wars of Insurgency

Two weeks into Operation Restore Hope a strange irony of history was evident. As the last of the eight feeding-center cities was being secured, the Italian army moved into Gailalassi, as the French had into Baidoa and the Americans into Mogadishu. Three decades earlier this was a wholly different Italian protectorate. Somaliland was also a remaining vestige of a colonial era, and in a panic like the world had witnessed in Saigon, US personnel were hastily evacuated from the American embassy in Mogadishu.

Ethiopia, as we know from the Acts of the Apostles (8:26), was an early center of Christianity. Alexandria and other North African cities were centers of theology and philosophy. In the summer of 1992, as starvation and the immanence of intervention in Somalia drew near, the pope left Italy for Angola. At Ciampino Airport in Rome he was asked by Italian reporters, "Why does the pope always go back to Africa?" What does this pope say? Here is one who has held that spiritual and moral chaos was bringing the world to the brink of political collapse. What does he say here and in central Africa where in some countries one of three persons is infected with HIV? This pontiff who has asked for restoration of family life, celibacy in the ministry, and the "sanctity of unborn life" offered this astounding claim:

> . . . throughout his seven-day journey, he insisted in his homilies that the essential character of the people before him was religious, however much they had been perverted by Marxism and materialism, slavery and war. The continent he said, was the birthplace of values and culture "in its original—and, yes, primitive—sense."[4]

In one of the ultimate and compounded ironies of history, Christianity expanded from its oriental cradle across the north side of the Mediterranean Sea and into the vast environs of the old Indo-European world, Europe and Russia. Leaping over Arabia and Africa, it left a fertile spiritual seedbed for Islam beginning in the seventh century. After that historic evasion of opportunity, Europe and Russia—centers of Roman, Orthodox, and Protestant

---

4. Alan Cowell, "Challenge to the Faithful," *New York Times Magazine*, December 27, 1992, 11, 12.

The Heritage and Destiny of the Somalian People

Christianity—spawned the demonic ideologies of materialism, secularism, and Marxism, which it would inflict on this impoverished Third World through the terrible swords of colonialism and the Cold War. Jeremiah and Isaiah, the eighth-century prophets of Jerusalem, together with Amos of the Northern Kingdom condemned the moral declension of people as the transition from pastoral, shephardic life to urban commercial life laced with idolatry, inhumanity, and injustice. The ethical affliction of ancient Somalia is none other than this sort of biblical violence.

Throughout Somalian history, the dry months between January and March were occasions when the nomadic herders of camels and cattle migrated down into the coastal trading centers of Berbera and Seylar. Here at the annual bazaar, Asian traders would search for incense, ivory, ostrich feathers, and animal hides. Tradition holds that at least one of the magi drawn to Bethlehem for the birth of the Christ child came from Africa, perhaps having purchased the precious gifts at such a bazaar. But the African bazaars, like those in the Near Orient, are not only occasions of priceless purchase but times and places where everything has its price and everything is for sale. The ultimate degradation that drove Somalia to the verge of apocalyptic collapse was the Cold War version of the ancient bazaar where even a nation itself could be bought and sold in the marketplace.

Not only do religion and immorality flourish in the commercial center of the city, but anonymity encourages private and public exploitation. Amos, the shepherd of Tekoa, in prophetic wisdom similar to Somali poetry, condemns those who luxuriously recline on beds and houses of ivory, oppress the poor, crush the needy and sell the righteous for a pair of camel sandals (see Amos 2–3).

The context of the Isaiah passage that headlines this chapter is the crushing threat of Assyria and the Egyptian alliance on Judea. Covenantal fidelity, which is ethical righteousness, and the sublime sense of the divine lordship which tempers human arrogance, is the guarantee of blessing and prosperity. Injustice and exploitation call down divine wrath, often expressed as natural, economic, and political calamity. The severity and solemnity of being right and reconciled with God, fellow humanity, and the world echoes throughout the world as a song of cosmic harmony. In a similar way discord, disease, and drought accompany alienation and rebellion in a dread funeral dirge as it sullies and saddens the whole wide earth.

ETIOLOGY AND DESTINY

The Africa Watch Report of January 1990 is entitled *Somalia: A Government at War with Its Own People*. The report draws the peculiar juxtaposition which will raise the theme of homogeneity and heterogeneity to which we will later return. "There is a painful irony in Somalia's predicament. Internal conflict is tearing apart the one nation in Africa that is truly homogeneous—ethnically, culturally, and linguistically, a unity that has been strengthened by a common Islamic heritage."[5] This cohesive heritage now yields a chaotic present and an uncertain future. Perhaps hybrid vigor—even the diversified pluralism of modern secular states—is more conducive to peace than is harmonious unanimity.

We began this introductory chapter with a note about swords and plowshares. It is New Year's Eve as I write this reflection. The *New York Times* has featured a lead article on "Swords to Plowshares" in Bosnia. The evening news features the pleas of Bosnian Muslims to the United Nations to become "peace makers" and not just "peace keepers." If the Western powers and the United Nations want to help, they are saying, "Let them make peace" by confronting the warring, raping. and exterminating Serbs. "At least drop the arms embargo so that we can fight our own battle," they cry.[6]

In that same region on the same evening, the country of Czechoslovakia has bifurcated along the lines of old Bohemia, Moravia, and Slovakia. Why is it that freedom does not foster toleration and diversification but rather ethnocentrism, ethnic cleansing, nationalism, tribalism, and violence? Why do the

5. Human Rights Watch, *Somalia*, 1.

6. John F. Burns, "Bosina 1992: The Paradox of Swords to Plowshares," *New York Times*, December 31, 1992, A1.

The Heritage and Destiny of the Somalian People

victims of brutal Nazi atrocities now visit the same genocidal atrocity on Bosnians in Sarajevo or on 415 Palestinian leaders now exiled by Israel on the Lebanon border? Shouldn't Serbia and Israel know better? Doesn't history bear moral instruction? Is Israel perhaps correct and are Germany and Japan wrong? Pacifism may be passé and the rightful posture of once-beleaguered peoples should be constant vigilance and severe retaliation against the slightest provocation. Biblical ethics offers both threads. There is the belligerent ethos commanded to the land-invading and consolidating Israelites as they lay claim to Palestine and Trans-Jordan.

The New Testament alternatively commends pacifism as Jesus and Paul offer "turn the other cheek" and non-retaliation.

Just as a pastoral and tribal past has been thrown into crisis in confrontation with colonial and Cold War history, so Somalia's destiny will be shaped in the tension between a natural and a contrived future. If her natural heritage and organic patterns of life are allowed to flourish, she awaits a benign and promising future. The natural tribal patterns of elder authority have close affinity with the nascent freedoms now sweeping the African continent. If Somalia again becomes the pawn of global superpower machinations or geopolitical economic manipulations she awaits a bleak and parched future. A song in the peaceful, moist, and verdant night, or the wind drawing across the dead and dry waters of affliction—justice will mete out one or the other future.

In an editorial in the *Miami Herald* entitled "Hope in Somalia," new hope was expressed as Passover and Easter were celebrated in 1993:

> At long last, after decades of conflict, two years of anarchy and famine, and months of disquiet under a U.S.-led humanitarian force, Somalia may at last be nearing an end to its long ordeal. Its a faint hope, to be sure, but it's hope all the same.

Leaders of all 15 of Somalia's feuding factions have signed a peace accord intended to restore a stable government to their country within two years. . . . The next stage would convene a transitional national council to organize and administer the

Ethics and the Wars of Insurgency

government until a permanent governing structure is established by 1995. . . .

> Still, it has been a long time since Somalis dared to idle about the streets of Mogadishu, let alone celebrate with music and flowers. There's a long way between that and real, lasting peace. But it's a way that, at least for now, suddenly seems open and ready to be traveled.[7]

As spring breaks in Europe and North America, Botswani troops under UN flags replace US troops in Baidoa. A park for children's play had been built by the departing US Marines. It had been constructed from the debris of dismantled "technicals" which once spread terror through the streets. Discerning the shape of a more free, just, and peaceful future requires that we probe more carefully normative forces that shape the dialectics of judgment and redemption. We now turn attention to the parameters of history and biology in order to define those norms of constriction and possibility.

---

7. "Swords to Plowshares," reprinted in the *Chicago Tribune*, April 13, 1993, 1.18.

2

Nationhood and Anthropogenic Famine

How History and Biology Have Shaped the Somali Crisis

The noise of a multitude in the mountains, like as of a great people; a tumultuous noise of the kingdoms of nations gathered together: the LORD of hosts mustereth the host of the battle. They come from a far country, from the end of heaven, even the LORD, and the weapons of his indignation, to destroy the whole land. / Their bows also shall dash the young men to pieces; and they shall have no pity on the fruit of the womb; their eye shall not spare children. / Every one that is found shall be thrust through; and every one that is joined unto them shall fall by the sword. Their children also shall be dashed to pieces before their eyes; their houses shall be spoiled, and their wives ravished. / Therefore shall all hands be faint, and every man's heart shall melt. And they shall be afraid: pangs and sorrow shall take hold of them; they shall be in pain as a woman that travaileth: they shall be amazed at one another; their faces shall be as flames. (Isa 13:4–5, 18, 15–16, 7–8)

Ethics and the Wars of Insurgency

AFRICA IS A CONTINENT that has twice been visited by a powerful host from a far country. By the late nineteenth century, after the industrial revolution in Western Europe had created an insatiable hunger for materials and markets to stimulate production, Africa became a patchwork quilt of colonial investments. Now again, in the late twentieth century, visitors from far countries came to Africa seeking strategic Cold War interest. The turn of the millennium now witnesses the demise of Cold War power politics, the desire of Western nations to pervade Africa with the ambiguities of freedom—plebiscite democracy, multiparty government, human rights, and market economies. These exuberant and exhilarating forces play hard in societies that have been fashioned into autocratic rule, both by history and by our contortions.

Swords often pierce even the young and helpless before they are reforged and wrought into plowshares. The bleak hollowed eye sockets of famished children in the arms of their starving mothers are cruel symptoms of world where all "faint and grow weary as their hearts melt."

PAINFUL PILGRIMAGE: CLAN SOCIETY, AUTOCRACY, ANARCHY, DEMOCRACY

One of Somalia's ingenious poems says:

> If you don't know the country you will get lost;
> if you don't know the people, you will go hungry.[1]

The geography and gastronomy of Somalia intertwine. From recorded history hers has been a history of hunger. Political leanings and loyalties are always laced with the subject of subsistence. The yearning for subsistence has often made Somalia prey for foreign intervention. In 1860, just as the American states struggled with its first international moral anguish of global industrialization and commercialization—the Civil War—France was the first

---

1. "Somalia Saying," quoted in Lee V. Cassanelli, *The Shaping of Somali Society: Reconstructing the History of a Pastoral People, 1600-1900* (Philadelphia: University of Pennsylvania Press, 1982), 9.

Nationhood and Anthropogenic Famine

foreign power to gain a foothold in Somalia. This was followed in 1887 by the British protectorate in the northwest and the Italian colonization of the coastlands in 1892. After the decades-long holy war to expel the foreigner-infidels, Italy's presence prevailed, and Somalia became a banana republic under Mussolini. More benign trusteeship followed under the United Nations from 1950 until British and Italian Somalia were united into the independent state of Somalia in 1960.

The first impulse for modern Western Christians to go to Somalia is expressed in Sir Richard Francis Burton's adventure diary, *First Footsteps in East Africa*. The adventure was animated not by Livingstone's missionary ideal or Henry Stanley's commercial interest, but the sheer delight of discovery. Burton first described Tanganyika, the greater of Central Africa's lakes. Looking back with contempt on Victorian English civilization, the young aristocrat who had been "sent down" from Oxford at his own instigation to join the India Army sought gates east of Eden and primal paradise. He was a scholar of Islam, as well as Arabic, Persian, and several Indian tongues. Starting at Aden in 1854, his exploration, under the auspices of the East India Company and the India Army, would take his entourage to Lake Tangenyika by 1858. At this time, to the rest of the world Somalia was *terra incognita*.

Burton's stated purposes of the Somali excursion begin to cast light on the historical crisis that haunts us to this day. His exotic journey, replete with hundreds of camels, is one reason that 140 years later marine frogmen would swim ashore at Mogadishu that strange December night:

1. Describe the geography, anthropology, languages, ecology, etc.

2. Proffer civilization: ". . . the Somal [an "essentially commercial" people] have lapsed into barbarian by reason of their political condition . . . but they appear to contain material for a moral regeneration."[2]

---

2. Burton, *First Footsteps*, xxx.

Ethics and the Wars of Insurgency

Burton goes on to chronicle the moral preferability of the Somali to the Arabs, whose influence he feels has been degrading. He speaks of the lack of respect the Somali now have for the British, evidenced in piracy, murders, and general disdain for presumed British authority. Western curiosity about the inferiority imputed toward African peoples—these mentalities embodied even in one as enlightened as Burton—have sullied Somalian history and have come back to haunt us in the frightened eyes of today's dying children.

The social and cultural disruption occasioned by this reverse visit of the magi is seen as Burton describes a day among the Eesa, a northwestern tribe:

> The life led by these wild people is necessarily monotonous. They rest but little—from 11 P.M. till dawn—and never sleep in the bush, for fear of plundering parties. Few begin the day with prayer as Moslems should: for the most part they apply themselves to counting and milking their cattle. The animals, all of which have names, come when called to the pail, and supply the family with a morning meal. Then the warriors, grasping their spears, and sometimes the young women armed only with staves, drive their herds to pasture: the matrons and children, spinning or rope-making, tend the flocks, and the kraal is abandoned to the very young, the old, and the sick. The herdsmen wander about, watching the cattle and tasting nothing but the pure element or a pinch of coarse tobacco. Sometimes they play at Shahh, Shantarah, and other games, of which they are passionately fond: with a board formed of lines traced in the sand, and bits of dry wood or camel's earth acting pieces, they spend hour after hour, every looker-on vociferating his opinion, and catching at the men, till apparently the two players are those least interested in the game. Or, to drive off sleep, they sit whistling to their flocks, or they perform upon the Forimo, a reed pipe generally made at Harar, which has a plaintive sound uncommonly pleasing. In the evening, the kraal again resounds with lowing and bleating: the camel's milk is all drunk, the cow's and goat's reserved for butter and ghee, which the women

Nationhood and Anthropogenic Famine

prepare; the numbers are once more counted, and the animals are carefully penned up for the night. This simple life is varied by an occasional birth and marriage, dance and foray, disease and murder. Their maladies are few and simple; death generally comes by the spear, and the Bedouin is naturally long-lived. I have seen Macrobians hale and strong, preserving their powers and faculties in spite of eighty and ninety years.[3]

Contrast that serene passage with this from Africa Watch testimonies of governmental brutality against its own people in June of 1989. Samia Sheef, interviewed by Africa Watch in London on June 3, 1989, told of the devastation caused by the bombing campaigns at Annayo:

> We knew that the bombing had already started in Hargeisa and Gebiley. One day we heard loud speakers coming from an SNM car warning the people about the bombs. Suddenly, from the direction of the wind, we heard a piercing noise. There was panic. Some people instinctively threw themselves on the ground, while others ran in all directions, only to be chased by the planes. The first plane had obviously been sent to get a sense of the settlement. Then the second plane came to drop the bombs. They flew very low. The first to be hit were two young girls. We became demented with fear. My children were not with me; they had been looking at a vehicle. I became terrified at the thought of my children being hit by the bombs. I started to inch towards them, but I couldn't move much because of fear of the bombs. There was some everywhere and people suffocated. Everyone started to choke. As the bombs dropped relentlessly, children started to wet themselves from fear. Many suffered diarrhoea immediately. Many adults and children couldn't stop vomiting. The noise was piercing. Children clung to you and wouldn't let go no matter what you did to shake them off. It was as if they had lost their reason...
> . When the bombing ceased for awhile, people came back, shaking themselves as if they had just in a trance.

3. Ibid, 179–82.

Ethics and the Wars of Insurgency

some pregnant women went into premature labor. Mohammed Guled's wife, only six months pregnant, lost the baby.[4]

Interested and disturbing external presence can eventually lead to internal chaos. After Burton's visit and the colonial involvements that would ensue, a twenty-year "holy war" against the colonizers followed. Led by Sayid Muhammed Abdille Hassan, the campaign from 1900 to 1920 was sporadically instigated by various tribes. Hassen is today remembered as the "Father of Somali nationalism." Two decades may again be needed for nationalistic reconstitution after the collapse of Cold War machinations, the tribal uprising against President Barre, and the reassertion of tribal antagonism during the anarchy of the early 1990s.

The former director of Africa Watch, Somali Rakiya Omaar, sees Somalis slide into anarchy caused by the collapse of the clan system. The only hope for the reconstitution of a viable people is the revival of a vital clan system in every village, town, and region throughout the land. Only when these age-old methods of decision-making and problem-solving are restored will any semblance of order return.[5]

FAMINE

We have used the sociological trade word "anthropogenic" to describe the Somali famine that has precipitated, in part, the present scourge of mass starvation. History shows us the coincidence between the fighting and famine. By July of 1992 Siad Barre's forces had evacuated Mogadishu. The former strongman was now exiled in Kenya. War lord Aidid, whose fortress and stockpile of weapons had to be dismantled in the first military clash of Operation Restore Hope on January 7, 1993, still struggled with stragglers of Barre loyalists and conflicts moved into the north. By that time

---

4. Author's paraphrase of Sheef's testimony from the interview.
5. Liz Sly, "Somalis Dare to Dream of Reconciliation," *Chicago Tribune*, December 28, 1992, 1.12.

Nationhood and Anthropogenic Famine

famine had begun to take its toll because of two failed harvests. People had no jobs or money. Rural areas had been looted and scavenged and farmers were forced by the fighting to leave their land. A bitter cacophony of destructive forces now sang together a lament heard round the world. With the US and UN presence gone by early 1992, it became of the voice of the voluntary relief agencies—Care, World Vision, Oxfam, Save the Children, and the like—that would cry out to the conscience of the world.

Writing in the *Chicago Tribune*, Liz Sly reflected on the tribal-pastoral heritage as it responded to famine throughout the ages:

> In days past, these clans roamed the desert with their camels and their goats, seeking out water holes and grazing lands. The stronger tribes protected the weak, who paid tribute to the warrior clans in return for peace and access to resources. At times of drought and famine, conflict was inevitable, and wars flared. But they were formalized battles, fought with swords and spears and rarely lasting more than a week. When it was all over, the elders came together to negotiate compensation and divide the spoils. The victorious clan gave the vanquished clan virgins to bear new sons to replace the men who had been lost. [Contrast this with Serbia's eugenic policy of mass rape in Bosnia.] Peace was cemented with blood ties, and the equilibrium was restored.[6]

Famine intensifies rivalry. Famine forces patterns of frugality and cooperation. Famine is exacerbated when responses of greed and violence displace patterns of sharing at best and profiteering at worst. Throughout the centuries, herds served Somalians as disaster insurance. Famine incites the best and worst in human beings. When people can hold something back, have something in reserve, they have leverage and negotiating power. When persons are reduced to abject impoverishment, they become desperate and resort to any means of securing resources. In the cities of America, inmates in prison will sometimes say, "I had nowhere else to turn. Robbery was the only course left open to me."

6. Ibid.

Ethics and the Wars of Insurgency

Somalian technicals, the remaining entrepreneurs of that society, say the same: "Give me a job and I'll stop stealing and selling the food intended for relief." Ironically, when a society becomes savagely inhumane, even men in jail will say, "At least here I have a warm bed, three square meals a day and healthcare." But what a price to pay.

FAMINE AND HUNGER

Just as human attitudes exacerbate or ameliorate famine, human injustice is often the root cause of hunger. An underlying thesis of this book is that injustice necessarily provokes strife and justice is the underlying precondition of peace. Hunger in particular and famine as a more complex ecological-political phenomenon is also often the outgrowth of deliberately inflicted injustice or negligent failure simply to "do justice." Hunger and poverty predictably emerge out of certain social structures. In Somalia, for example, exploitation has engendered hoarding (even stealing from NGOs), which has provoked scarcity and subsequent starvation. The fact that two thirds of the world now lives in desperate poverty is not the result of an intention of those 10 percent of the world's population who posess 90 percent of the world's wealth to impoverish the rest, but the necessary side-effect of concentrating wealth and resource in that one sector.

In the colonial period, Western nations such as Spain, France, and England felt the need for raw materials to supply their emerging industrial capacity. The English came to Carolina, the French to Africa, and the Spanish to Mexico to exploit such resources. The primary intention of these colonial incursions was not to destroy. In fact, colonialism sought to civilize and edify the peoples it visited. But 90 percent of the aboriginal population in Mexico and North America was exterminated in the process. What James Beckett observed in the case of Mexico may again become the case in Somalia:

Nationhood and Anthropogenic Famine

Millions died in the collision by disease, by warfare, and by the fracturing of viable economic units.[7]

What is the gene sequence of anthropogenic famine in Africa? Though many subtle steps were involved, something like this sequence occurred:

- Africa is defined by the developed West as a "supplier" of primary products such as agriculture, minerals, etc. Remuneration is contrived as low as possible through price fixing and market manipulation.
- Even in the indigenous land, resources of the many are expropriated by the few.
- The arms race becomes the vehicle to control markets.
- The subsistence base of local economies and the participant bases in global economies collapses.

As I write these words on January 13, 1993, America, France, and Britain have launched another air attack on several Iraqi surface-to-air missile installations. Still in power two years after the Gulf War, Saddam Hussein is experiencing the severe effects of embargo and sanctions imposed after the war. Declaring a new Jihad, a "holy war" against the West, he appeals to the deeply felt legacy of American and Western intrusion into the Arab world.

How ironic that deep in the night of January 12, as American pilots took off toward southern Iraq from bases in Saudi Arabia while not far south, in the horn of Africa, American Marines were seeking to secure food lines to feed starving Somalis. Here the American presence seems to make a policy statement of commitment and help; there a statement of intimidation and destruction.

UN and US policy intently and intensely seeks to impoverish and even eliminate Iraq. We deliberately sought to destroy infrastructure—bridges, communication networks, sewer systems, health systems—during the Gulf War. After the war, sanctions and

---

7. James Beckett, "'The World Economy: Short on Change,'" in *The Development Apocalypse, or: Will International Justice Kill the Ecumenical Movement?*, ed. Stephen C. Rose (Risk 1, 2; Geneva: World Council of Churches, Youth Department, 1967), 13.

Ethics and the Wars of Insurgency

embargo were imposed which threatened the population's access not only to arms and technological goods, but to food and medicine as well.

American foreign policy regarding Iraq is deeply conflicted. In order to assuage our guilt over the Holocaust, we have made profound and historic commitments to Israel seeking to assure that no strong Arabic or Islamic adversary will emerge in the Middle East. Iraq now and Iran later will fall under this Damoclean sword. We seemed to be possessed by a virulent rage that would stop at nothing—would falsify facts and ignore all truth and justice in our abhorrence of Saddam Hussein. It seemed like a sublimated self-loathing that we had toward ourselves.

Famine is an instrument of war and genocide. Throughout history genocide-imposed starvation has been involved in contrived famines such as Stalin's famine in the Ukraine in 1932. Famine ensues when the agricultural rhythm and structure is disrupted or destroyed. Famine ensues when growers are driven from their lands or when food delivery mechanisms are neglected. The challenge of a transition from peace-making to peace-keeping in Somalia will require the restitution of indigenous farming processes.

International news recently told the story of an enterprising woman farmer who was growing maize, which she could not then move into market because the price had collapsed because of the surfeit of donated grains through the volunteer agencies. In the late twentieth century, when most vestiges of barter economies are gone, the blessed and sustaining processes of food exchange are inextricably intertwined with economics, technology, and politics.

Feeding, fasting, and famine are also sacramental phenomena. The religious significance of bread and hunger, the religio-ethical imperative to feed the hungry and the socio-political mandate to eliminate the condition of anthropogenic famine are theological and transcendental matters as well as humanistic and secular matters. The great spiritual texts of all faith traditions equate bread with the very essence of divine sustenance. President Bush has referred to the forces in Somalia in messianic terms as messengers of peace. After the bombing of Iraq, he said in a press conference on January

Nationhood and Anthropogenic Famine

14, 1992, "The world is safer today because of the courage of those who did the Lord's work yesterday." The most fundamental imperative of the "Lord's work" is to share bread for the world. This is the meaning of Eucharist, of gratitude and thanksgiving in all ethics. The starvation of children is in extra measure unconscionable. Drawing on the deepest spiritual traditions of Christendom, Dr. Martin Luther King Jr. proclaimed at the march on Washington in 1963 that "undeserved suffering is redemptive." The hundreds of thousands of children who have died in Somalia are redemptors. They have vicariously been sacrificed for the sin of the world. Their excruciation (crucifixion) will save the world.

Writing in the *New York Times*, Sylvia Nasar shows that famine is not, as Malthus thought, "Mother Nature's revenge on hapless humanity." It is most often not a drama of natural calamity such as drought or adverse weather conditions. Famine is "a manmade disaster, an avoidable economic and political catastrophe.... Disaster strikes because the poorest, most downtrodden members of society suddenly can no longer afford to buy food, usually because of sudden unemployment or a surge in food prices." Nations or international entities that are conceived to avert or ameliorate famine can do so by deliberate decision and action. "In the 4th century B.C., a Sanskrit book advises: 'During famine, the king should make a storehouse of foodstuffs and show favor to the subjects or institute the building of forts or water works.'" The EPA and other works projects were not just "make-work" endeavors but carefully conceived plans to save victims of the Depression from degrading hopelessness and starvation. "In 1846–1851, Ireland starved in the potato famine largely because Parliament would not raise English taxes to save it, though it raised $60 million for the Crimean War."[8]

The millions who died in the avoidable biblical scourges of famine and war are not examples of salutary trimming of the weak to strengthen healthy stock by weeding out the vulnerable in some kind of Darwinian or Malthusian mechanism—these are

---

8. Sylvia Nasar, "It's Never Fair to Just Blame the Weather," *New York Times*, January 17, 1993, 4.15.

Ethics and the Wars of Insurgency

temptations to test how the race will choose either care and creativity or selfishness and lethal neglect.

Just as it might be acknowledged that although the population of states within the former Soviet Union appear now to be much closer to starvation than they were under the totalitarian regime, their plight falls far short of the starvation and famine facing Somalia, Ethiopia, and the Sudan and large portions of Africa. Poor peoples have often collapsed into rude and insensitive totalitarian regimes just when the opportunity for democracy and societal flourishing became real.

In the present political and economic tumult gripping all of Africa, it will be crucial judgments when we decide whether human rights, free press, pluralistic toleration, and democratic process will become our national and global priorities. If sounder policies do take hold the chances of subsequent famine will be greatly diminished. Nasar concludes:

> History suggests that America's mercy mission won't solve Somalia's starvation problem. Stable governments let farmers grow and democracy helps protect the poor.[9]

---

9. Ibid.

3

Ecology and Economy
Apocalypse and Hunger

The paper reeds by the brooks, by the mouth of the brooks, and everything sown by the brooks, shall wither and perish, be driven away and be no more. (Isa 19:7)

THE MESSIANIC ECOLOGY OF Hebrew Scripture speaks of the transience of both natural and fabricated sustenance. In our actions we sow the seeds that either nourish or sicken. We reap what we sow. "Plant a radish—get a radish." Sometimes we sow well and still reap destruction. Natural law is no trump card over divine justice. The Lord blesses or curses whom he will. Human power is always at its best tenuous. Our experience of transience and fragility intensifies our ethical obligations to feed the hungry, shelter the homeless, heal the sick—attend the "least of these."

As Dr. M. L. King Jr. described his political agenda, prophetic ethics is "non-aggressive physically but dynamically aggressive spiritually."

Ethics and the Wars of Insurgency

The Bible affirms this simple ethical truth: If we can only shun injustice and achieve justice in the world, God's reign of peace will ensue. Jews believe that the moment perfect justice is manifest in this world, Messiah will appear. With belief now colored by the apocalyptic and eschatological curtain, a curtain separating that serene expected ultimate from this shattered experienced penultimate, Christians believe that incognito gestures of genuine compassion penetrate the veil and mimic, even invoke, that impending kingdom:

> "When did we see you hungry and offer you food?" . . . "In as much as you did it to one of the least of these, my brothers, you did it to me." (Matt 25:37, 40, paraphrase)

Though our temporary tabernacles (tents) in this world are like paper reeds, here today and gone tomorrow, we are called to construct and build. As we have done in Somalia we are called to construct tents and tabernacles for the homeless and uprooted. We are commissioned and commanded to build provident households for the human family. The mechanisms by which we do this are the household edifices of ecology and economy (from the Greek *oikos*).

But our domicile is precarious. Life and health are stolen from us by the brutish and non-discriminating forces of nature—earthquake and drought. We are robbed of existence and well-being by forces of nature to which is added human malevolence thereby yielding a particular virulence—famine, disease, war. Life and safety are stolen by sheer human violence—stealing, starving, killing.

In the *New York Times* of January 24, 1993, Alison Mitchell wrote of the "Fifth Horseman of Somalia: Stealing":

> Marauding gangs, many organized by warlords and merchants, cut down telephone cables and dug up electric wires for the copper inside. They tore up the streets to steal the sewer pipes, leaving sewage to pour into the

Ecology and Economy

streets. . . . Economists, bloodlessly, call what happened disinvestment.¹

AK-47s supplied the continued violence of the clan and warlords. An unnamed Pentagon official commented on December 4, 1992, "Between the stuff the Russians and we stuck in there during the great cold war, there are enough arms in Somalia to fuel hostility for 100 years."²

The connection between ecology and economy, war technology and theology, is telling. In the state of Tripura in India, the original population of Buddhist and Christian inhabitants has been deluged by millions of refugees from Bangladesh and East Pakistan. These refugees have fled both natural ecological disaster and the impoverishment of famine and loss of the natural aquifer. This extrusion, then intrusion, has generated conflict, high and low tech, which threatens the fabric of this region.

The same interplay of forces is seen in Somalia. Here, the famine can be traced, in part, to what one writer calls "God's Gunboats."³ When President Bush sent troops into Somalia in late 1992, he drew on the rhetoric of Holy Crusade, saying the mission was to "ease suffering and save lives" and to rescue from death "thousands of innocents." His sermon concluded, "So, to every sailor, soldier, airman, and marine who is involved in this mission, let me say you're doing God's work. We will not fail. Thank you, and may God bless the United States of America."⁴

Firmly rooted in the tradition of Woodrow Wilson, who saw the eradication of injustice and squalor and the achievement of peace as the divine destiny of this nation, George Bush and Bill Clinton continue to affirm the manifest destiny of America as

---

1. Alison Mitchell, "Fifth Horseman of Somalia: Stealing," *New York Times*, January 24, 1993, 4.

2. Quoted in Richard J. Barnet, "Still Putting Arms First," *Harper's Magazine*, February 1993, 61.

3. Lewis H. Laphan, "God's Gunboats," *Harper's Magazine*, February 1993, 10.

4. George H. W. Bush, "Address on Somalia," December 4, 1992, online: http://millercenter.org/president/speeches/detail/3984.

Ethics and the Wars of Insurgency

that of saving the world, sending out counter-cowboys against the apocalyptic riders. Just as Israel's "Holy War" in the late second millennium B.C. was sacred cultic activity as well as an expression of "Yahweh's sovereignty over history" (Mendenhall), so in the late second millennium A.D., the citadels of power of Christendom now recapitulate a pagan idolatry as well as the legitimate purposes of justice.

The US would guard the gates east of Eden and not allow any Iraqi invasion of Paradise (the forbidden and cordoned off fruit was now oil). The emblazoned sign in the sky to prevent reentry would be squadrons of F-15s and self-imposed "no-fly zones." But now atoning sacrifice had to be made for Abel's blood spilled in the dirt. Now in Somalia we would offer atoning sacrifices of meal and grain, water and milk, tincture and bandage—the sacraments of salvation. As Lewis Laphan wrote:

> By redefining the balance of power as the peace of God, the new world order recasts the military establishment as quasi-religious organization (unless circumspect gays are suspect) and provides them with the permanent tasks of salvation.[5]

Like God, the new world order reserves the right to decide which of the innumerable evils that stalk the planet (apocalyptic horsemen) deserve punishment or correction.[6]

This becomes a circuitous come-around to the four horsemen of the apocalypse—white, red, black, and pale—which are associated in biblical tradition with political strife and war, famine and disease. These horsemen symbolize the inscrutable and inevitable powers of scourge and disestablishment at work in the natural world and in the divine judgment and economy. They also symbolize the seemingly intractable and unavoidable forces of human malevolence, exploitation, and thoughtlessness, the vicious abrogations against natural and divine order. Like Knute Rockne and the famed "Four Horsemen" at Notre Dame University in 1915,

5. Ibid., 12.
6. Ibid., 13.

Ecology and Economy

the world powers, particularly the US and the USSR in recent generations, have poised and positioned intimidating military force before the rest of the world in order to assure and secure political advantage. We have also armed nearly every nation on earth in hope of receiving the payback of beholden loyalty in the economic and political competition.

When the economically impoverished Somalia turned from the Soviet Union after 1977, the US singlehandedly bolstered the fragile Somali army and security forces with massive military and other aid, totaling over one billion dollars. In Somalia, this power became an authority to repress the citizenry just as our massive aid to Iraq in the next decade would validate Saddam Hussein's repressive regime. With this support, Siad Barre built a large stockpile of military hardware and trained hundreds of thousands of young men in its use. It is this modem arsenal of US-supplied rifles, TOW anti-tank missiles, 155-millimeter Howitzers, along with the infamous Soviet-provided AK-47s, which now haunts the world. Now we can ask, why Somalia and not Sudan? What of Haiti and Bangladesh? The desperately poor and famished are found in various places. Shouldn't international largess be equitably designated and administered? The exertion of politicized justice is always tinged with arbitrary selectivity and aggrandizing self-interest.

The apocalyptic specter portrayed in the rich imagery of Revelation 6 is a poetic vision of the natural and supernatural judgments. Justice, as we understand it, in secular or spiritual meaning, involves amending past and present wrongs and avoiding future wrongs. Judgments are the inevitable working out of "reaping what has been sown" (Gal 67:7), of the present concealed sin "finding us out" (Num 32:23), or of the impending judgment being delayed by repentance and emendation of life (Jonah 3:2ff.).

The judgments of God and the world are held in check by the grace of Christ as the expression of God's mercy. As Jacques Ellul has written, the calamities envisioned in Revelation 6 are judgments on history, judgments which have been, are now, and will be judgments "which would have had to be but for the redeeming and forgiving power of the intercession of the immolated lamb."[7]

When Oliver Stone uses the composer Samuel Barber's song "Agnus Dei" as the haunting background music to his movie *Platoon*, he suggests apocalyptically that a transcending sympathy and sacrifice drops back as a veil behind historical violence, bearing redemptive power within those violent events.

> Truth forever on the scaffold, Wrong forever on the throne,—
> Yet that scaffold sways the future, and, behind the dim unknown
> Standeth God within the shadow, keeping watch above his own.[8]

The four horses are the forces of history. White and red, black and pale, their interwoven threads form the rope of history. This ligature of judgment binds the world back to its primeval bliss (*religare*: religion) and forward to its ultimate purpose. The white horse, symbolizing the word of God, is the divine justice and mercy that suffuses all of history. Evil is evil because of the messianic thread in history. Without God, there is no theodicy problem. Evil just is, unless there is some imputed purpose in the universe.

> I watched as the lamb opened the first of the seven seals. Then I heard one of the four living creatures say in a voice like thunder, "Come!" I looked, and there before me was a white horse! Its rider held a bow, and he was given a crown, and he rode out as a conqueror bent on conquest. (Rev 6:1, 2 NIV)

The one who rides the white horse is "faithful and true" (Rev 19:11). The "winds of revenge" (Sir 39:28-31) that gallop in the wake of the white steed convey judgment, but that justice is

---

7. Jacques Ellul, *Apocalypse: The Book of Revelation* (New York: Seabury, 1977), 146.

8. James Russell Lowell, "The Present Crisis," quoted from *Yale Book of American Verse*, ed. Thomas Raynesford Lounsbury (New Haven, CT: Yale University Press, 1912; online ed., Bartleby, 1999, http://www.bartleby.com/102/128.html).

Ecology and Economy

ordered toward his saving purpose. Judgment is a call to repentance, authenticity, and fulfillment. Take Somalia: As the world observed the sad tragedy of children dying from natural and contrived famine, it was conscience-stricken. Theologically construed, the world fell under the pale of divine judgment. Justice, at the human level, simply means amending past wrongs, ameliorating present evils, and avoiding future harms. Doing justice in the biblical and humanistic sense is seizing the possibility for good in a crisis. Judgment is an occasion for rectitude which has at least the dimensions of correction and safeguard.

The red horse of Revelation 6 symbolizes war. War is the perversion of the divinely given political power possessed by the state. Power is apportioned to states to order, achieve justice and peace. Distorted power becomes aggressive and aggrandizing. When the sword of justice is misused for war, elicit punishment has been transmitted into revenge or humiliation. The January 1993 bombing of Iraq to "teach Saddam Hussain a lesson" is such an abuse of power. War in Somalia and Bosnia in early 1993 reflects the same injustice. The feuding factions that seek to consolidate their power, maximize their cache of contraband weapons, frustrate popular access to food and the requirements for living, and generally terrorize and brutalize the people are examples of justice distorted to corruption. Similarly, in Bosnia, with the Serbian forces' occupation of villages and regions, ostensibly to protect Serb minorities, came destruction of libraries and mosques, refugee deportation, rape centers, and concentration camps, unbridling the flaming red horse of evil:

> When the Lamb opened the second seal, I heard the second living creature say, "Come!" Then another horse came out, a fiery red one. Its rider was given power to take peace from the earth and to make people kill each other. To him was given a large sword. (Rev 1:3–4 NIV)

When the previously peaceful Roman Empire began to lose cultural excellence and authority and became bellicose, it turned to vicious antagonism and repression of its polyglot peoples, especially the Jewish and Christian sects with their subversive loyalties.

Ethics and the Wars of Insurgency

This historical experience of persecution informs the ethos of the Book of Revelation.

> When the Lamb opened the third seal, I heard the third living creature say, "Come!" I looked, and there before me was a black horse! Its rider was holding a pair of scales in his hand. Then I heard what sounded like a voice among the four living creatures, saying, "Two pounds of wheat for a day's wages, and six pounds of barley for a day's wages, and do not damage the oil and the wine!" (Rev 1:5–6 NIV)

The black horse symbolized famine. During the siege of Jerusalem instigated by the Roman general Titus in A.D. 70, vineyards and olive groves were ordered not to be destroyed. Nevertheless, the Roman purpose until the last ramparts of Massada were overrun was to famish this recalcitrant people. Economic scourge is the ultimate apocalyptic weapon to devastate a people. The unconscionable evil of stealing food from starving babies in Somalia reenacts the magnitude of this evil.

When people get weak, they get sick. In the wake of famine, pestilence stalks. When the United States and its partners decided to embargo Iraq and bomb, we willed and acted to kill the populace by destroying their infrastructure. Our stated purpose was to "bring Iraq to its knees" with the hope that it would then topple its now-demonized president. The starvation and sickness of Iraqi children after the war has been a burden of continued disgrace on the victorious Western powers.

> When the Lamb opened the fourth seal, I heard the voice of the fourth living creature say, "Come!" I looked, and there before me was a pale horse! Its rider was named Death, and Hades was following close behind him. They were given power over a fourth of the earth to kill by sword, famine and plague, and by the wild beasts of the earth. (Rev 1:7–8 NIV)

4

Just War and International Law
Axiology and the Search for a New Morality of the Common Good

Say ye to the righteous, that it shall be well with him: for they shall eat the fruit of their doings. Woe unto the wicked! It shall be ill with him: for the reward of his hands shall be given him. (Isa 3:10–11)

Woe unto them that join house to house, that lay field to field, till there be no place, that they may be placed alone in the midst of the earth! (Isa 5:8)

IN BOSNIA IT IS genocide. Villages are systematically cleansed of their inhabitants. The women are gathered into rape centers and to the invasion of hearth and home is added the womb. In Israeli occupied lands it is ecocide. Houses are laid side by side and Palestinians are displaced. Homes are invaded and leaders, doctors, professors, and priests are exiled out on the cold mountains of southern Lebanon. We create hell on earth. In his *Divine Comedy*

Ethics and the Wars of Insurgency

Dante depicted heaven and hell, the eternal drama of vindication and damnation that is symbolized biblically by the four horsemen of the apocalypse. We may surmise that in Dante's retributive vision the young thugs of Somalia who steal for themselves food designated for hungry children will surely sit in hell, welded to their technicals, with—like Bacchus of old—grapes, bread, wine, and love hanging just beyond their reach.

Nevertheless, beyond the frustration the grapes do ripen in due season. Because the power of justice is anchored in the righteousness of God, we can have confidence that justice will beget peace even as falsehood and violence will lead to calamity. Rooted in this primal sense of right, wrong, and recompense depicted by Dante a, moral sensibility has developed across the ages. It is embodied in Greek mythology and philosophy, as well as in Hebrew ethics, Roman civil justice, and Christian compassion. It eventually yields a heritage of just-war theory. The doctrine is part of a richer fabric of custom which normatively contemplates the proper role of the sword in the hand of the state. Ethically derived law moves through three stages: theocratic, autocratic, then democratic. Developments in this evolving tradition of natural, national, and international law point us toward a time when the power of states will no longer be used, as one cynic said, "to kill people and break things," but to insure human rights, feed the starving, and pacify warring parties, among other humanitarian goods. This archaic ethical heritage which we find in both Orient and Occident assumes its modem and universal expression in the medieval tradition of *jus ad bellum*—the causal justification of war. Classical theory found seven reasons and conditions necessary for one nation to intervene against another. Here is my own paraphrase:

- That people must seek defense against exterior (and on rare cases interior) attack.

- Rightful authority (like a president, senate or United Nations) must call for the intervention.

Just War and International Law

- Right intention must animate the intervention (not teaching Saddam Hussein a lesson, or protecting our political interests or maintaining the flow of cheap oil).
- The goal of the intervention must be restitution of peace.
- The evil (suffering, destruction, death) must be proportionate to the good to be achieved.
- There must be a reasonable hope of success (e.g., the hesitancy to invade Bosnia despite the genocide occurring there).
- The intervention must be a last resort (all other initiatives must have failed).

Several ingredients are found here that justify a humanitarian use of military power in Somalia: The aggressor is the scourge of starvation, precipitated and accented by the hands of violent tribal belligerents. The United Nations endorsed the initial intervention and is committed to safeguard the achieved peace (if member states like the US will only pay their delinquent dues). Although some suspect ulterior motives such as enhancing one's political influence in the Horn of Africa, the intention of our intervention in Somalia comes close to the unalloyed good of saving lives. While the goal of Western intervention is the restitution of peace, we are not sufficiently cognizant of our own role in creating the disequilibrium in the first place. Nor are we aware of the enormous task entailed in restoring a pastoral polity and economy to a people who must now exist in this modem world of frantic economic competition and global interaction. Peace (*shalom*), as we have shown, is hard to come by. It can only be built on the sure foundation of justice. It is not merely the contrived avoidance of strife.

Dr. Shawki Sabri, Deputy Minister of Health in Iraq, speaks of the ensuing chaos when imposed peace is disjoined from justice. Iraq, he claims, "is suffering severe shortages of medicines, surgical instruments, and birth control devices." The Western coalition "first destroyed the Iraqi infrastructure, then our water, fuel, electricity and sewage systems." "Its illogical, inhuman and

Ethics and the Wars of Insurgency

it violates medical ethics."[1] The extraordinary US and Western efforts to rebuild Germany and Japan after Dresden and Hiroshima are expressions of magnanimous justice that create more "perpetual peace" (Kant). Contrast this to the humiliating after-effects of imposed sanctions such as we laid on Germany after WWI or Iraq after the Gulf War.

> Woe unto them that join house to house, that lay field to field, till there be no place, that they may be placed alone in the midst of the earth! (Isa 5:8)

When we impose no breathing space, no latitude on the vanquished or impotent, we only breed simmering resentment and the craving for revenge. This revenge eventually lashes back.

But justice, not facile acceptance, must be done to make ready for peace. "All too frequently the rush to end a conflict and find peace has resulted in impunity for the perpetrators of crimes."[2]

Professor Bassiouni, of DePaul University, a member of the United Nations Commission of Experts to Investigate International Law Violations in the former Yugoslavia, raises a crucial point with reference to justice in Bosnia-Herzegovinia. The Geneva Conventions and other international humanitarian laws have been sorely violated by the Serbs in Bosnia. Ethnic cleansing, forced rape, violating or harming innocent civilians, disregarding the sick, and abusing prisoners all are violations of the Geneva Conventions and international law. Those who have ordered, committed, or condoned these crimes must be brought to justice before there can be peace.

As I write, it is Friday, February 12, 1993. It is Abraham Lincoln's birthday. The powerful Civil War spiritual, rich in double entendre, is on the air waves: "We Are Coming Father Abraham 300,000 More."[3] Mr. Milosovich, the Serbian president, and Mr.

---

1. James Yuenger, "Iraq Doctor Laments Medical Shortages," *Chicago Tribune*, February 10, 1993, 1.5.

2. M. Cherif Bassioun, "War Crime Tribunal: The Time Is Now," *Chicago Tribune*, February 11, 1993, 1.29.

3. Words by James Sloan Gibbons (c. 1862).

Just War and International Law

Karadjzic, the leader of the Bosnian Serbs, have recently compared their aggression against Bosnian Muslims to Lincoln's Civil War against the insurgent Confederacy. One is tempted to be less than cordial and ask where these butchers who have created concentration camps, rape centers, ethnic cleansing, and the slaughter and deportation of mothers and children where they get off comparing themselves to Abraham Lincoln.

The force of evil and wrong creates a burden of guilt in the face of the moral universe and the righteous God who sustains life, death, and justice to that universe. This wrong must be recompensed and the guilt relieved. This process is the work of divine and natural judgment mediated through the mechanisms of human justice. An example: On December 18, 1992, the United Nations General Assembly established a war crimes tribunal (patterned after the Nuremberg Tribunals at the end of WWII). The European Commission, the Conference on Security and Cooperation, and hopefully the World Court will now draft the statute for such a tribunal. All this is to satisfy the *jus ad bellum* criteria of "rightful authority." Evidence will then be gathered, the case made, and judgment rendered. All this is somewhat unprecedented in the field of international law and policy. We have voluntary groups such as Amnesty International that research and document human rights abuses. Agencies like the International Red Cross and Red Crescent monitor humanitarian concerns during conflicts, but we lack the forceful mechanisms to condemn and punish with any authority apart from sheer national power. Even the Gulf War and the imposed sanctions on Iraq are only nominal in terms of international order. In the end it basically remains for the United States and some coalition of nations to enforce a peace.

As I write US diplomats are in Russia seeking to dissuade that government from supplying arms for Serbia's genocide in Bosnia. If a configuration of power perhaps can be forged, even one based solely economic enticements, then an international judgment might be exerted. The establishment of universal justice waits for the establishment of a universal ethical contract or covenant and some international body for implementation. The

Ethics and the Wars of Insurgency

world in this remarkable age, which has been called "the end of history," is slowly moving toward such an ethic. The articulation of the Nuremberg documents, the Universal Declaration of Human Rights of the United Nations, the Helsinki Accords, and the pronouncements of the World Council of Churches and the Congress of World Religions are moves in this direction.

What is the root source of our cultural ethics about law and violation, guilt, recompense and exoneration? The clearest articulation of this ethical-legal vision is found in the sequence of covenants received by the historic faiths—Judaism, Christianity, and Islam—that collectively constitute the Abrahamic heritage. When Abe Lincoln walked down the street in Springfield, Illinois, the little girl walking ahead of him stumbled and toppled back into his arms. Mr. Lincoln caught her, bore her up, and softly said, "Go home and tell your mom that you rested in the bosom of Abraham." The Abrahamic heritage, like the bosom of Abraham, the perennial recital of righteousness, which is the legacy of historic religion (i.e., religion grounded in creation and revelation/sacred writ), resonates with the moral imperatives of the other living religions of humanity (see Robert N. Bellah, *The Evolution of Religion: From the Paleolithic to the Axial Age* [Cambridge, MA: Harvard University Press, 2011]).

The dimensions or stages of covenant that ultimately ground universal ethics and international law are Noachic, Abrahamic, Mosaic, Levitic, and Christic. The Noachic covenant pertains to the whole world. The universal flood had yielded a second chance for the human race, Adam. Were it not for the cleansing rescue, the judgment of God and nature would have fallen on all life—the geosphere. Brother had killed brother and blood cried up from the earth. The ecological, ethologic harmony—the graceful reciprocity of humans with the creation and the creatures—had been violated. Now the covenant of life with life was reinstated, drawn with blessing and warning before the source of all life.

The Noachic covenant, though formalized late in the history of Israel, represents an archaic and primal understanding of divine and natural law derived from earlier societies in the Ancient Near

East (Assyria, Babylonia, etc.), such as it was understood that blasphemy, idolatry, adultery, animal cruelty, and murder were proscribed. *Biritu* (Akkadian), *berith* (Hebrew), and *diatheke* (Greek) are words that point to this fundamental sense of moral destiny and obligation. As history unfolds, this moral apprehension becomes the basis of all social contract, constitution, and legislation. Genesis 9 and Job 5:23 are texts where we find this primitive tradition embedded. In the Abrahamic covenant (Gen 15, 17), a newly perceived pilgrim deity promises a nation and generativity to a people in exchange for their exclusive devotion and trust. Symbolized by the bisected animal sacrifice, this covenant is profoundly earnest as the Abrahamic setting of animal and child sacrifice (infanticide) would attest. Abraham is called to a particular and universal people, "as the sand on the seashore" (Gen 22:17). The ultimate horizon is established which Paul the apostle will later recall at Athens.

> He made out of one nation [*ethne*] to live on the whole surface of the earth, having fixed times and boundaries of their habitation. (Acts 17:26, paraphrase)

The ethical significance of the Abrahamic covenant is that we are given in life an allowance of freedom, opportunity, habitat, and benefit in return for our commitment to non-violence, faithfulness, fairness, and helpfulness to the needy. Land and rights are the divine allotment contingent upon stewardship and responsibility.

The Mosaic covenant is thought by modem scholars to be the pattern of social and religious organization in the Late Bronze Age. The covenant's objective was the maintenance of justice and peace within the community. The form of the Mosaic covenant (Deut 29, Exod 15) was patterned on the international treaties prevalent at this period in the Ancient Near East. Treaties of the Hittites and Assyrians which have come to light in recent years contain all of the elements that we find in the Mosaic covenant. Murder, theft, adultery, false oaths and accusations, injustice, insubordination of children, and schism are all anathema before God and violations of inter-human justice. These breaches in human order are

Ethics and the Wars of Insurgency

ruptures or tears on the solidarity and community that is at once transcendent *shalom* and secular law and justice—perquisite to human concord.

The Levitical or holiness covenant adds a vital dimension to a comprehensive ethic and perhaps unexpectedly to the realm of national and global legality and polity. War is a matter of cleansing, especially ecologically animated war, such as Iraq's invasion of Kuwait to protest Kuwaiti horizontal drilling into the Rumalia oil field and America's counterinsurgency to protect its oil interest. Genocide, such as that occurring in 1992, is fathomable only as a violation of holiness ethics. All ethics have a dimension concerning contamination and purification. Rabbis can only consecrate Israeli troops for conflict at certain times and under certain conditions. Undoubtedly, modem secular states, including Israel, will go to war with no precondition if it is expedient. The universal aspect of the holiness ethic is given by the ubiquity and unavoidability of death; death inspires dread and awe—the experience of the mystery of the holy. Circumcision was the seal of the Abrahamic covenant (cf. Gal 5:3). In the history of war, chastity has often been the requirement of the warrior. This background is the subconscious source of resistance and ultimately of receptivity to the newly proposed acknowledgment and authorization of gays in the military.

The most fundamental feature of the Levitical covenant is that all human being and action takes place before the reality of God. The most fundamental aspect of the nature of God is holiness and righteousness. This inescapable presence places on humans the requirements of purity and justice. This God is the ultimate warrior and peace-maker and the only justification for war is what has been delivered as holy war, just war, and jihad—not human violence, pride, or retribution.

On the theme of this volume, one cannot witness the sordid international events of 1992 and 1993 without noting the presence of Gog, anti-Gog, and antichrist. There are symbolic and parabolic representations of the deeper impulses of good and evil, transcendence and immanence, which we encounter in war and peace. The ultimate refutation to the required cultic purity of warrior and

Just War and International Law

citizen is *porneia* and genocidal rape. This is the final defilement. It is tragic evidence of the degradation of the soul of Western Christians, Muslims, and Jews that we are not told or will not hear the Muslim tale of defilement from the system-authorized genocidal rape of Bosnian Muslim women. It would require an education into the holiness traditions of Abraham which we share for us to understand the horror and blasphemy of that brutality. So, rather than face our damnable selves, we refuse to see and hear what is happening.

Can rape be a weapon of war? Is it part of the spoils? Homeric booty? Killing the flower of male youth of the enemy—and life goes on, or begins again. Rape defiles and degrades the mothers of all living beings, inflicting irreparable shame and enduring wounds. The shame and disgust of the modern war sequence—Somalia, Srebrenica, Rwanda—has seared the human soul with collective horror. "In the Balkans," writes Lance Morrow in *Time Magazine*, "ethnic purity is a primitively overriding value. Bosnian Muslims believe that the mass rapes are intended to break down their national, religious and cultural identity . . . the greatest debasement is to pollute a person's descent."[4] A final mutation occurs in the notion and configuration of covenant that deeply affects political and military history. The coming conquering kingdom comes to be envisioned as otherworldly.

"The kingdom of God is within you" (Luke 17:21). "My kingdom is not of this world" (John 18:36), said Jesus of Nazareth. The holiness priests and eschatological prophets had spoken of a day when a new spirit, a new messianic reign, would be implanted in the hearts of the faithful. Jesus was far from a Maccabean nationalist and restorationist. He disappointed Judas and all the sword-wielders of his day. His donkey ride on Palm Sunday, as the 1964 New York World's Fair film *Parable* depicted, was a charade packed with judgment.

The primitive New Testament community was deeply pacific. The ethic of non-retaliation and "turn the other cheek," which was

---

4. Lance Morrow, "Unspeakable: Rape and War," *Time*, February 22, 1993, 49.

Ethics and the Wars of Insurgency

intensified by an apocalyptic demonization of the Roman Empire especially before the fall of Jerusalem in A.D. 70 and through the episodic waves of severe persecution, dominated Christian conviction, at least until the conversion of Constantine in A.D. 325 and Augustine's defense of Christendom against Barbarian invasions in the early fourth and fifth centuries. Even in his day as church leader in North Africa, the great bishop-theologian was ambivalent on the question of whether a Christian could go to war.

The Christic covenant, the covenant of grace, repositions hope in eternal life and in the transcendent God, rather than in political utopia. Apocalyptic and eschatological covenant is also worldly. The spirit of forgiveness and reconciliation is implicit in this faith, and hope and charity creates the foundation of an ethic that will seek peace and justice among nations. This forgoing sequence of covenants undergirds a sacred and secular tradition of just war which forms within Judeo-Christian-Islamic civilization. Augustine relates this covenantal political theology to the threatened Roman Empire surrounded by Barbarians. Aquinas appropriates it in the late Middle Ages to an age of incipient nationalism in the West when Eastern Christendom had already withdrawn into autonomy. Maimonides and Ibn Sina add their nuances, and Juarez and Grotius take the same theological covenant and relate it to new enterprising tendencies of global circumnavigation in Renaissance Spain and Holland. Nineteenth- and twentieth-century Europeans and Americans apply a sense of covenantal manifest destiny to geopolitical expansionism and imperialism. In all of these epochs a covenantal theology has undergirded a just-war political ethic.

To conclude this chapter, let us review two positions on just-war theory that move toward "swords into plowshares." Michael Walzer's conclusion in his landmark book *Just and Unjust Wars: A Moral Argument with Historical Illustrations* (New York: Basic Books, 1977) explores the political viability of a non-violence response to aggression and war. Former President Jimmy Carter presents the rationale, now embodied by the Carter Center, to prevent war and conflict by deliberative negotiation and reconciliation.

Just War and International Law

Walzer replays the scenario offered during the Cold War and nuclear buildup by Bertrand Russell and other "ban the bomb" pacifists in England and elsewhere. What if a country declares a war and no one comes? What if one party invades another and no one offers resistance? This passive resistance rooted in the grace covenant of Christ was exemplified by some Christianized Indian tribes in North America. Like the gleeful martyrs in the Roman Coliseum or the silent Jews herded like sheep into the gas chambers, these Amerindians were summarily executed and exterminated as they probably would have been had the aggression been joined.

When non-violent resistance, as exemplified by Gandhi or Martin Luther King Jr., confronts aggressive force, it is either obliterated or, as in the Salt March, it exhausts the aggressor and thereby wins the day. In Walzer's scenario, the citizens simply absorb the invasion. The invading force has to keep the life-support systems going by cooperation or coercion, otherwise it would have to import everything—food, water, energy, communication, etc. Eventually, through weariness the aggressor is silenced unless, as is happening in some sections of Bosnia, the entire region is depopulated, ethnically cleansed, or deported into some no man's land. Passive absorption of aggressive evil is a latter-day recapitulation of early Christian pacifism. When viewed in light of the absurdity of all-out nuclear war and the contemporary military reality of the near-perfect ability to simulate outcomes, the moral position becomes practical and realistic. In the long run, such historical judgment may find Iraq the victor of the Gulf War.

Former President Jimmy Carter is promulgating an even more conceivable and possible program to activate this new mutation of "just war." The Carter Center now monitors the 115 wars going on in the world. Through negotiation and arbitration of conflict, the Center has already effected settlement in places like Nicaragua. Through hard, respectful, economically disinterested, ethically grounded confrontation and negotiation, and with a military power like the US or some coalition of forces to secure and stabilize, striving parties are moved toward reciprocal recognition

Ethics and the Wars of Insurgency

of rights, plebiscite participation, and achievement of democratic structure and justice-grounded peace. Mr. Carter believes that those who have power, influence, resources, and provisions should put on their blue jeans and tool belts, go out there to points of need, and rebuild, supply, and restore.

Carter's strong and programmatic reconciliation is more fitting to the political dynamics of the end of this millennium than is the pacifism of non-resistance. In the spirit of the might and magnanimity with which with the Allied powers twice withstood the destructive force of Germany, Arnold Toynbee anticipates a new model of world leadership:

> What the situation manifestly demands is a voluntary association of the peace-loving peoples of the world in sufficient force and cohesion to be unassailable by any who reject their pact of collective security or who break it; and this peace-keeping world-power must not only be sufficiently preponderant in strength to make attacks upon it hopeless; it must also be sufficiently just and wise in the use of its power to avoid the provocation of any serious wish to challenge its authority.[5]

In this spirit the morning news (February 19, 1993) carries a story that gives new meaning to the messianic text, "A little child shall lead them" (Isa 11:6). A group of Somali children led American soldiers to a burial ground in Mogadishu where they found six Russian surface-to-air missiles stashed away. We have planted our gardens of destructive enmity and the earth has yielded her bitter fruits.

As gardens again grow in Somalia and UN peace-keepers assume jurisdiction in this despoiled paradise, Leonard Bernstein takes the theme of Voltaire's *Candide* to proffer a song of hope. The world once again has the choice to either sow to destruction or plant the seeds of justice, care, and peace. His concluding chorus is memorable:

---

5. Arnold Toynbee, *War and Civilization* (New York: Oxford University Press, 1950), xi, xii.

Just War and International Law

And let us try before we die to make some sense of life. . . . We'll build our house, and chop our wood, and make our garden grow.

EXCURSUS: CONFESSION

I have never been in the Horn of Africa and the continent's northeastern section—but again, I have always been there. As a divinity student in the 1960s I sailed into Alexandria, executed a few sketches of this dramatic and historic horizon, dreamed of the tragic fire in that harbor that incinerated the treasured texts of antiquity, stayed a few days, then went on to Beirut. This first touch-down on that ever so bright "Dark Continent" was followed some years later when I landed in Tangier, Morocco, with a hope of travelling along the south Mediterranean coastlands of North Africa, which I have written about so often even up to recent essays on Tunisia, Libya, Egypt, and the dynamisms of the "Arab Spring."

Today many of my students are in Africa. In Kenya and Liberia, Uganda and South Africa, more than a dozen masters and doctoral scholars with whom I worked on conflict issues ply their ministry with distinction. Three of my students were members of Mandela's South African leadership cabinet. Peter Mageto, now dean of the theological faculty in Nairobi, Kenya, prepared a fine dissertation on HIV and the religious bodies in Africa—Christian and Muslim. Another student, Daniel Wanabula, is Methodist bishop of Uganda and Kenya, with mission interests stretching over to Somalia in the ecclesiastical jurisdiction of East Africa. Though I have been discouraged from venturing into Somalia right now (even though I've assured them that my ransom from kidnappers would never merit a fee much more that $10), these dear friends in ministry and education are never out of my mind and heart.

Twenty years ago, when I retired from teaching in the medical world of Chicago and moved into theological education in two distinguished global institutions—Garrett-Evangelical and

Ethics and the Wars of Insurgency

Cambridge—I started writing on ethical issues in the Middle East and Africa. The core of this work focused on those stirring events we associate with the film *Blackhawk Down* in 1993. This represented a radically new departure for my professional work and is resonated today when our son, a pediatric geneticist, practices his research and patient care in places like Egypt, Qatar, and India.

The lecture homilies you read in this book brood on the land of Mogadishu—the land of the kings and magi and the aromas of frankincense and myrrh.

5

Ethnic Eviction
Fratricide And Genocide:
Anthropology, Psychology and Violence

Have ye not known? Have ye not heard? Hath it not been told you from the beginning? Have ye not understood from the foundations of the earth? (Isa 40:21)

IN 1731 THE PROTESTANT minority was evicted from the Roman Catholic ecclesiastical principality of Salzburg. Earlier in the 1560s the same Calvinist/Lutheran minority—including my ancestors in Belgium and France—were evicted or exterminated because of their faith. In 1755 the French Catholic population was expelled from Acadia. Need we mention the kindred faith-murders and deportations of Jews and Muslims across the centuries? Today (2013) we hear that the Kurds have been offered certain ethnic status in Turkey—hope is never totally overwhelmed by human wickedness.

Then, not to be undone, the aforementioned seventeenth-century Euro-Americans slowly sought to exterminate the

Ethics and the Wars of Insurgency

Amerindian populations of the "New"—their old—world. Beginning in 1992, Bosnian Muslims were systemically removed from their villages in the Caucasus and left to wander and resettle as refugees—this five centuries after they had been removed by the Catholic kings from their European homes. Ethnicity may exacerbate rather than reconcile in Bosnia. The ancient people of southern Slavia are one people ethnically. The cleansing or exterminating comes from a religious impulse. In 1054 these Eastern peoples had become Orthodox. Roman Catholicism prevailed among what were then known as the Croats. The Bosnians converted to Islam under the Turkish influences in the Ottoman Empire.

To continue the geopolitical saga as it relates to Somalia: There in 1993 General Morgan led his tribal contingent against enemy tribes in Kismayu. In light of this cultural history the ironic danger of biblical "beating swords into plowshares" (or "plowshares into swords"; Isa 2:4/Joel 3:10) comes into focus. We may disarm one tribal group in Somalia only to insure that they will be exterminated by another. We can impose an arms embargo against the Bosnian Muslims and insure that they will be overwhelmed by the weapons-rich Serbians. After the events in Somalia came the Balkan events and eventually the events in Iraq, Afghanistan, Syria, and Iran—all exhibiting the same ethical hazard and ambiguities. Today (2013) in Armenia and especially Ngorno-Karabak, Azerbijian, Muslims are seeking to exterminate the inhabiting Orthodox Christians by means of siege, starvation, and direct killing. Meanwhile, in Sudan a Muslim military government is beginning the slow genocide of Christians in the south. In Bosnia, Croatia, and Slovenia more prosperous Catholics or Muslims are under siege from the envious and less affluent Serbs to the south. Turkey is calling for a concerted attack by Western powers against Serbia. As I update this twenty-year-old work in 2013, streams of weapons are carried by Saudi and Qatari planes into Turkey to arm the Syrian rebels against the farsighted president-ophthalmologist Assad—a mass-murderer of his own people. American, British, and Western powers still quiver in fear at some resurgence of the Muslim conquering world which once occupied her southern

Ethnic Eviction

flanks as well as the aggressions of the Turk-Ottoman Empire. The ghost of global crisis haunts the psyches of East and West as they remember the cultural disgrace and devastation of the Muslim conquests and the reactive Crusades of the Western European church. The memory is near unbearable as it issues in the legacies of the attempts of Christian civilization to eradicate Jews and Muslims from the world—culminating in the Shoah, which nearly accomplished that demonic and blasphemous desire.

At Easter season of 1993 I met in Oxford with a leader of the British military department who wanted to challenge my view that NATO or America should intervene in Bosnia. His view was that military ethics first required that one's own soldiers be protected and not be futilely sacrificed. Perhaps now, he hinted, the older impulse of expelling and eliminating the enemy under some doctrine of religious hegemony had now transmuted into narrow self-survival purposes.

A scholarly seminar at the University of Chicago today (1993) seeks to debunk the notion that primitive humans were not warlike and that primitive warfare was relatively ritualized and, for the most part, benign. Does strife and violence belong to the inherent instincts of human beings and are the warrior virtues part of the nobility of the human family?

The Prussian military philosopher Helmut Von Moltke dissented from Kant's vision of "perpetual peace":

> Perpetual Peace is a dream—and not even a beautiful dream—and war is an integral (*ein Glied*) of God's ordering of the universe (*Weltordnung*). In war, man's noblest virtues come into play: Courage and renunciation, fidelity to duty and readiness for sacrifice that does not stop short of offering up life itself. Without war the world would become swamped in materialism.[1]

In Thornton Wilder's play about the human drama of war and peace, *The Skin of Our Teeth*—for which I was in college typecast as Mr. Antrobus—the big generic Man endures through

---

1. Quoted in ibid., 16.

Ethics and the Wars of Insurgency

generations and aeons from creation and flood—from war(Cain and Abel) to modern deluge—trying to assuage chronic aggression and transfigure its energies into reconciliation and peace. Sabina the daughter of Antrobus—the fickle embodiment of the "pleasure principle"—cries out in petulance as civilization lies in ashes and ruins, "Mr. Antrobus, I hate to see the war end. People are at their best in war-time."

Toynbee argues that the primitive aggression unleashed in violence has been intensified and concentrated in world history in two phases: First, the religious wars of the sixteenth and seventeenth centuries, which finally ended by the establishment of a spiritually grounded doctrine of toleration. The Treaty of Westphalia was a critical turning point in this history of religiously prompted strife. Then came a new history of the wars of nationalism which culminated in the two World Wars of the twentieth century. If Toynbee were alive today he would see some one hundred wars underway in various parts of the world—from Bosnia to India to Lebanon and Azerbaijia. These conflicts represent a woeful admixture of these two great epochs prior to and after the "Peace of Westphalia."

In my argument, "religion" is a binding-back to originating and unifying sociocultural constitution—one both worldly and transcendent. Just as persons ask, "Who am I ?" and "What should I become?," religions ask, "What people are we?," "To whom do we belong and owe our corporate life?," "What constitutes our community?," and "What ligatures bind us ethnocentrically to our own and ecumenically to other people?" Why does Saddam Hussein continue to shell and gas his own people, inflicting on them unspeakable cruelty and violence? Why does he attack the Shiah in the South and Kurds in the north? Has the Western incursion and occupation—ultimately Abu Grahib and relentless killing of hundreds of thousands—also severed the cords that bind? Why have Somalian tribes turned on their own, seeking their starvation and extermination? Has our intervention helped the crisis or exacerbated primal associations and covenants? Have we so disturbed this ancient land—her primordial justice and camaraderie—that we have brought lethal antagonisms despite our good intentions?

Ethnic Eviction

"Tribes are movements of people where a coalescence of race, religion, and identity comes to shape economic history."[2] Joel Kotkin's words signify the depths of meaning providing the secular foundation to the theological meanings of the Book of Acts: "God has made of one blood all nations, setting the bounds and times of their habitations..." (17:26, paraphrase).

The world is a network of association crisscrossed by labor and capital. The peoples that survive and thrive—Jews, British, Asian Indians, Japanese—find ways to turn these markets to their advantage. Existence becomes a process of securing livelihood for you and yours while not transgressing or impeding the same initiative in others. This search for economic well-being, for household vitality, is intimately related to the genetic and evolutionary impetus to survival.

Perhaps war-making transmuted into work-making is the way that the Creator of all life on earth transfigures the world into a global household (*oikumene*).

In early March of 1993, Senator Sam Nunn of Georgia, a leading expert on military matters, proposed legislation that would have the armed services provide humanitarian programs at home and abroad. Relief work in weather related calamities, inner-city programs to help young people, environmental efforts by the army engineers corps would as in China become domestic services to the beautification and enhancement of all the people. This seemed like an enormous win-win program—helping conscripts to feel that their work was rewarding and bringing about tangible benefits for your sponsoring people.

This was the issue in late spring of 1993 when Operation Restore Hope in Somalia was renamed Operation Continue Hope. United Nations troops, often called "peace-keepers," replaced American regulars. Famine was soon checked. Only a few died daily while before it had been hundreds. It was thought that a new paradigm might serve the world well in Bosnia. The fratricidal wars seemed so futile and unwarranted and it seemed that

---

2. Joel Kotkin, *Tribes: How Race, Religion and Identity Determine Success in the Global Economy* (New York: Random House, 1993), 17.

Ethics and the Wars of Insurgency

everyone wanted someone to stand in the breach giving all an escape from a violence that all hated and from which all sought reprieve. As Gandhi sadly confessed, if "eye for an eye"—even that ancient Hammurabic advancement of bloodlust where one hundred lives were taken to revenge the loss of one of one's own—is to be the rule, we'll all end up blind.

At this point in our analysis it becomes clear that we are forwarding anthropological reasoning. Is the human condition one of perennial and inescapable violence or are there potentialities for goodness, justice, forgiveness, and kindness, and how do our appraisals determine our political actions? Our estimations can be idealistic, pessimistic, or some mediating realism. Do adversaries only respond to power and strength and deterrence or can moral suasions like reason, right, justice, mercy, and fairness come into play? If "might makes right" is our operational ethical dictum that we may be condemned to an ultimately hazardous outcome—winning the battle but losing the war? While Reinhold Niebuhr may be correct in finding "love" a virtue impossible to apply in political or military matters, it may be that Ghandi and Dr. King are correct in a deeper sense in their wager that non-violence ultimately is validated by the large arc of justice and peace in the universe, the substance of human conscience or the ways of a God of righteousness in world affairs—even in matters of economics, the politics of nations, or issues of war and peace.

EXCURSUS: HOLY WEDNESDAY 2013

Rabbi Herschel Schacter died this week. On Passover in April 1945 he entered newly liberated Buchenwald and cried out, "*Shalom Aleichem, Yidden—ihr sint frei.*" The corpses and near-dead and thousands of skeletal children seemed to rise up and vacate that den of demonic human cruelty. Biblical history had been reenacted as God's beloved children on Passover had once been exposed to slaughter. Today I join these in weeping. "I crucified the Lord—God's Son." I crucify him afresh as through my communities and political representatives I deny some of my human brothers and sisters the right to love one another and marry. I also expose the children of my nation to lethal exposure to millions of guns. I tell many friends that they cannot make their home here even though they have lived here all of their lives. Every day I crucify afresh the beloved Son through whom God so loved the world that he gave this gift. I weep and am chastised by the words of a seven-year-old resident of Buchenwald to young Rabbi Schacter: "I'm older than you, anyway. . . . Because you cry and laugh like a child. I haven't laughed in a long time, and I don't even cry anymore."[3] Today on Holy Wednesday and tomorrow on Passover and Maundy Thursday I'm aware that I've grown so old.

Two pieces of journalism represent the metaethics of the foregoing reflection and of the abrupt disclosure above. A pessimistic metaphysic is found in Diane Schemo's essay entitled, "Declare Victory, Hand Off, Slip Out, Cross Fingers."[4] The title portrays a confession of the moral legitimacy and therefore efficacy of the operation. Recalling that President Bush Sr. called on the world to "take a moral stand" and prevent warlords from keeping food from the two million persons threatened with starvation, the article acknowledges the difficulty verging on impossibility of restoring lost social structure and governmental order to this politically decimated nation. Like a mischievous boy who has stuffed all his junk in the closet and jammed the door shut, we creep out of the room fearing the cascade that will fall when someone opens the door.

In the same mood, Erich Olfert asks that we "Don't Call Somalia Intervention a Success."[5] The head of the African Central Committee of the Mennonites reminds us that famine had already peaked in Somalia nearly a year before Americans arrived and that massive infusion of foodstuffs may have not only fed the starving but had the unintended consequence of destroying markets for farmers. Recognizing and favoring the warlords and even the

---

3. Margalit Fox, "Rabbi Herschel Schacter Is Dead at 95; Cried to the Jews of Buchenwald: 'You Are Free,'" *New York Times*, March 26, 2013, A17.

4. *New York Times*, May 2, 1993, A1, 4.

5. *New York Times*, May 12, 1993, A10.

marauding youths in the intervention may also have undermined the natural authority of clans and elders.

On the other side, pessimistic social ethics disavow the prospects of building an earthly utopia and any kind of idealist transformation of our finite societies. In this view the estimate of the human condition tends to emphasize ignorance, ubiquitous malevolence, and conflicted motives in all human actions. We may work for reconciliation and peace but its perfect realization will always elude us under the conditions of existence. Yet we dream on and press on. This ethical and political perspective inclines toward "balance of power" politics, holds to a rigorous philosophical and practical doctrine of punishment and human constraint, and expects a final retribution where "your sins will find you out."

In the war in old Yugoslavia, for example, Savenka Drakulic writes to condemn the present posture of the European community against an intervention which in essence hangs people out to die in a kind of "exposure" to the consequences of one's sins:

> Astonishment gives way to anger, then resignation at the way Europe perceives this war—'Ethnic Conflict,' 'ancient legacy of hatred and bloodshed.' In this way, the West tells us, you are not Europeans, not even Eastern Europeans. You are Balkans—mythological, wild, dangerous Balkans. Kill yourselves if that is your pleasure. We don't understand what is going on there, nor do we have clear political interests to protect.[6]

In some measure the US withdrawal from Somalia abandons the future to the desires of irascible peoples who deserve the calamity they will inevitably receive. Like a frustrated parent who can no longer control or guide a willful or wayward child, the frustrating one is abandoned to its fate.

A more admirable attitude than hightailing it out in retributive rectitude is one that believes and seeks reconciliation and restoration. This realistic posture, which should have been taken earlier now by the West, now yields to an international protective

---

6. Slavenka Drakulic, *The Balkan Express: Fragmentation from the Other Side of War* (New York: Norton, 1993), 17.

presence that includes peace-keepers from the region. Now we can deal honestly with hostile factions as they cool down and take measure and distance—at the same time examining the centuries-old animosities that continue to irrationally break out in violence.

Moral realism holds that humans are capable of good or evil, altruism or exploitation. Such a stance seeks a creative tension between freedom and coercion in societal governance and policy. In Somalia this ethical orientation will try to reestablish equilibrium among warring tribes. Writing in the *Chicago Tribune*, Liz Sly finds hope in this approach: "Somalia's slide into anarchy and chaos was rooted in the collapse of the clan system."[7] Reconciliation therefore would require some recovery of these historic processes of consensus building and conflict resolution.

Geopolitical decisions are also shaped by idealist considerations. Realism, at least in the Niebuhrian sense, often underestimates the human capacity for dialogue and betterment. Views of political democracy believe that freedom, human rights, justice and peace can work if they are given a chance. This is true also for Marxist political systems and for the political derivatives of the Abrahamic and other world religions. Compassion and justice can assume efficacy in human relations when even national and political structures if they are put to the test. In game theory the Golden Rule maxim seems to often be verified when the rules require respect and reciprocity.

Christopher Joyner, a political scientist at George Washington University, reflects on this approach to issues in Somalia, Cambodia, and Serbia:

> Some countries are beginning to crumble and their peoples are looking to outside forces for help. Somalia, Sudan, Liberia, Cambodia and the former Yugoslavia are all failed nation states.[8]

---

7. "Somalia Dares to Dream of Reconciliation," *Chicago Tribune*, December 28, 1992, 7.1.

8. Christopher C. Joyner, "When Human Suffering Warrants Military Action," *Chronicle of Higher Education*, January 27, 1993, A52.

Ethics and the Wars of Insurgency

The humanitarian concern to alleviate human suffering is one of the finer impulses in the human spirit—individual and collective. Joyner concludes:

> If humanitarian intervention succeeds in Somalia the UN will have taken up a new mission. Not only will the Security Council work to maintain peace and international security but it will use military intervention to make this happen.[9]

This has proven to be a new development in the international structures and processes seeking to ameliorate human anguish and enlarge peace among peoples. This is a fulfillment of the long yearning of the human race for ways to avert discord and violence and establish justice and peace. This leads us in our unfolding argument to scan the future horizon to find there the theological and moral (eschatological and ethical) corroborations of these political imperatives and possibilities.

9. Ibid.

6

Theology, Polity, and the Pacific Vision

Futuristic Hope, Pastoral Restoration, and the Glimpse of a New World Order of Human Rights and Fulfillment

> Ye shall go out with joy, and be led forth in peace: the mountains and the hills shall break forth before you into singing, and all the trees of the fields shall clap their hands. (Isa 55:12)

WHEN THE PRESS AND media sought to interpret the meaning of the United States and United Nations sending military personnel to pacify and feed Somalia in late 1992, they often cited a biblical passage from Isaiah: "they shall beat their swords into plowshares . . ." The broader passage envisions a time of justice and peace when "nation shall not lift up sword against nation, neither shall they learn war any more" (2:4). This millennial and eschatological text invites juxtaposition with one of a more apocalyptic tenor from Joel, "Beat your plowshares into swords . . . ," which also has

Ethics and the Wars of Insurgency

its broader context: "Proclaim this among the nations: prepare for a holy war! I'll bruise the warriors!" (3:9f., paraphrase).

These texts have particular valence in the history of Israel. They reflect the pacifistic or militaristic bias of particular events in a particular moment of history. In the complex prophetic wisdom of Judaism, Yahweh can be seen to require might in order to issue peace (fight for the peace of God) or to demand peace as the reason to justify strife ("I will fight for you"/declare peace). The same prophetic scriptures are known by heart and recited by heart by both Ariel Sharon and Martin Buber. These involve the history of traditions of theological "just war" (holy war, pacifism, crusade). Apart from the peculiar historical context, these texts also have meaning for universal history and for the ethical inclination and disposition of the broader human family. In the haunting power of these scriptures, Dan Rather of CBS News shudders at the "apocalypse now" as he holds the hand of an injured child on his first night in Baidoa, Somalia, and he exalts in the words "swords beaten into plowshares" as a Marine helps a child in Mogadishu carry home his water. Kipling captures the mood:

> GOD of our fathers, known of old—
> Lord of our far-flung battle-line—
> Beneath whose awful Hand we hold
> Dominion over palm and pine—
> Lord God of Hosts, be with us yet,
> Lest we forget, lest we forget!
>
> The tumult and the shouting dies—
> The captains and the kings depart—
> Still stands Thine ancient sacrifice,
> An humble and a contrite heart.
> Lord God of Hosts, be with us yet,
> Lest we forget, lest we forget!
>
> Far-call'd our navies melt away—
> On dune and headland sinks the fire—

Theology, Polity, and the Pacific Vision

Lo, all our pomp of yesterday
Is one with Nineveh and Tyre!
Judge of the Nations, spare us yet,
Lest we forget, lest we forget!

If, drunk with sight of power, we loose
Wild tongues that have not Thee in awe—
Such boasting as the Gentiles use
Or lesser breeds without the Law—
Lord God of Hosts, be with us yet,
Lest we forget, lest we forget![1]

As Kipling knew, colonial expeditions and exploits across the seas toy with both mystery and menace. My exploration now moves deeper into the world-historical meaning of the *Blackhawk Down* moment in world history. What inferences of universal meaning can we draw from this momentary episode in 1992–1993? It certainly had something to do with humanity's struggle to formulate just and appropriate strategies of intervention into other nations. It also pertains to what we've come to believe about legitimate peace-making and peace-keeping—which all "high" religion finds to be an obligatory task. Each religion of Abraham, as well as the social derivative structures of these faiths in institutions—such as the United Nations, international law, the European Union, and in particular world powers such as Israel, the Arab League of Nations, and the United States—come into play.

The poem by Kipling not only speaks of colonial duty and interwoven divine mandates, it reflects an age when nations were called on for supererogatory works—feeding the starving and sacrificing lives as part of national and pan-Christian responsibility to the far corners of the world. These dominions of Christ were under our care as divine charge. My reflections will not so much ponder these highly ambiguous challenges but normal philosophical and

---

1. Rudyard Kipling, "Recessional" (June 22, 1897), quoted from *The Oxford Book of English Verse*, ed. Arthur Thomas Quiller-Couch (Oxford: Clarendon, 1919; online ed., Bartleby, 1999, http://www.bartleby.com/101/867.html).

Ethics and the Wars of Insurgency

humanitarian norms such as human rights and basic human needs arising from this particular set of crises in places like Somalia, Bosnia, and Rwanda.

INTRODUCTION

I began this work in 1992 with reflections on what is now called the "failed incursion" into Somalia. When America recently decided to play a part in humanitarian aid to Zaire following the massive dislocation of Rwanda's people in late 1996, the editor of *The Economist* wrote:

> Memories of American deaths in Somalia ... contributed to American hesitation. But in the end the humanitarian imperative once again is dragging in the armies of the rich, even before their screens have been filled with images of disease and death among the 1m-plus refugees in eastern Zaire. Zaire is no Somalia, but the core of the mission, protecting humanitarian aid in a war zone, is similar. The rest of the world may want to see starving children saved, but this is not necessarily a priority for the region's governments, rebels and warlords.[2]

As previously noted, I began my reflections on Somalia shortly after publication of my *Ethics and the Gulf War*. In that book I questioned the wisdom and righteousness of that adventure while hoping that national and international forces and resources today might be better used for peace-making and peace-keeping. Little did I know that this specific and complicated mandate and not swift surgical strikes (as in Iraq) or the Falklands would actually become military imperatives in the last decade of this war-fraught millennium. Now at the end of a sabbatical research leave from my teaching and Ethics Center leadership in Chicago, the challenge of Zaire has surfaced to dominate international news. Working in Strasbourg, France, the home of the European Parliament and its Center for the "Rights of Man " (Les Droits de'l'Homme), and

2. "The World Makes Up Its Mind(s) about Zaire," *The Economist*, November 16, 1996, 39.

Theology, Polity, and the Pacific Vision

collaborating with two of Europe's leading scholars on the theology of human rights—Jean Francois Collange in Strasbourg and Prof Ernst Fuchs in Geneva—has encouraged me to again open this file.

When I relocated from my post as Director of Bioethics at the University of Illinois College of Medicine to the new position as Professor of Theological Ethics at Garrett Evangelical Seminary and Director of a new Ethics Center at the seminary in concert with Northwestern University, such new themes commanded my attention. The Ethics Center started to develop an agenda on issues surrounding war and peace, rich and poor, and life and death. Working on matters of just-war ethics, economic ethics, and bioethics involved conferencing and publishing and thus proved worthwhile and an educational bonanza. We easily raised grants and endowments for the center. On our theme in this study we held workshops on Korea (with Bruce Cummings and Sam Moffatt, two pioneering theological and political thinkers). We proceeded to engage these communities (e.g., Presbyterian and Methodist Korean congregations) along with constituencies from Armenia, Bosnia, Israel/Palestine, and Rwanda. In the project on Bosnia, for example, we had leading scholars like Miroslav Volf of Croatia and large contingents of Serbian Orthodox, Bosnian Muslim, and Croatian Catholic faithful.

We sought to ponder the religio-ethnic strife presently underway in these ancient lands, to examine historical and causality factors, and to seek avenues for reconciling confrontation, mediation, and new pathways forward. We were happy to see how influential these Chicago communities could be across the world—back home. We emphasized critical dialogue with peoples who shunned natural contacts with these fellow religionists and countrymen. Real-time mediation with involved parties and then publication were found useful. In the Korean project, for example, wide numbers of women pastors and theologians were able to air their frustrations about access to ministry in patriarchal settings at home and abroad.

Ethics and the Wars of Insurgency

On our theme of Africa we welcomed our new university president—Henry Bienen, an Africanist from the Woodrow Wilson School at Princeton—to give his first lecture in his new home town. We looked at American policy in Rwanda and Burundi against the historical context of these critical matters. In Somalia, Muslim communities face crises exacerbated by the colonialism of the Christian West. In Rwanda, Burundi, and Zaire, Catholics, Protestants, and Muslims are engaged in life-and-death struggles creating grief for themselves and the broader world citizenry, agencies, and nations who seek to help.

As our argument has proceeded we have sought to set a broader context of nations for our tasks of deciphering and discernment vis-à-vis the values of meaning (theology) and morals (ethics). We have already related the saga of Somalia, at the Horn of Africa, to the Middle East and to Sub-Saharan Africa. We have seen how its secular history and biblical-hermeneutical history is related to the Balkans and Rwanda. The editors of *The Economist* speak of this larger fabric as the address the fast moving issue of Syria:

> After the first world war Syria was hacked from the carcass of the Ottoman empire [a blasphemous severing (Acts 17)?]. After the second [World War], it won its independence. After the fighting that is raging today it could cease to function as a state.
>
> As the world looks on (or away), the country jammed between Turkey, Lebanon, Jordan, Iraq and Israel is disintegrating. Perhaps the regime of Bashar Assad, Syria's president, will collapse in chaos; for some time it could well fight on from a fortified enclave, the biggest militia in a land of militias. Either way, Syria looks increasingly likely to fall prey to feuding warlords, Islamists and gangs—a new Somalia rotting in the heart of the Levant.[3]

If I'm given the strength (and presence of mind) on this evening of Easter I hope to further elucidate this interconnection by

---

3. "The Death of a Country," *The Economist*, February 23, 2013, 11.

Theology, Polity, and the Pacific Vision

tying present conflicts in the American foreign policy agenda—Iraq, Afghanistan, and Syria—into one complex tapestry. I will also ponder the meaning of the Boston Marathon event with its connection to Chechnya and the upper Islamic caucuses. The younger brother in that bombing confessed in a note he left in the boat in which he was hiding, "We did this to avenge the American killings of Muslims in Iraq and Afghanistan—killing Muslims somewhere kills us everywhere."[4] This will constitute a fifth volume of books on present wars—the Gulf War, Somalia, War on Terrorism, Arab Spring, and the new pieces now engaging world political policy.

The standpoint that I offer in all these reflections is that of religious ethics. At the same time I hope to explore with the reader not only the purview of theological ethics (Bible and faith), but the parameters of universal human rights and political-philosophical viewpoints. Today's mandatory secular biases, it is hoped, are actually complemented by my presumed "sacred" viewpoints. The peace-making processes in Bosnia, including war crimes tribunals, along with "truth commissions" and "forgiveness and reparations" rituals in Rwanda and in Mandela's South Africa, show the validity of such blended secular-sacred lenses. Such transcendental and ethical perspectives are necessary to a holistic view of the matters. Truth requires such imagination so as to not fall into a narrow economical or political reductionism on the one hand and religious reductionism on the other.

We live in a day of deep concern for ethical standards for human conduct and for renewed commitment to human rights. The brutal injustices and inhumanities that we have inflicted, such as harming and killing other persons, in this bloody century are unconscionable. We hope earnestly for a new millennium of peace as the sundial of history makes this epochal move. The pain had been pronounced:

- Racial conflict and killing
- Abuse and disrespect for women
- Neglect and violence toward children

4. CBS Evening News, May 10, 2013.

Ethics and the Wars of Insurgency

- Massive war and violence in violation of principles of civilian immunity

When the Jesuits or Belgian Reformed Protestants come to Rwanda they brought with them this doctrine of human worth. Regrettably, they also brought lessons of economic exploitation, education, and educational and cultural hegemony, including brutal violence—ethnic cleansing, tribal extermination, and genocide. Therefore the prophets live again. They are always contemporaneous. Every generation hears and kills them. Justice, for the prophets, is giving to every person what he deserves. To the prophets guilt is complex; if you are guilty all are responsible.

Still, from the ashes of these atrocities has arisen the phoenix of hope for human rights. These new commitments—including the war-crimes tribunals at the Hague; the formulations of global humanitarian rights in Geneva by the International Red Cross, Red Crescent, and other healing entities; the Universal Declaration of Human Rights and the whole cache of documents inclining the world toward peace as gathered by Dorothy V. Jones in her research at Chicago's Newberry Library (*Code of Peace*, 1989)—exhibit this development. This emergent body of materials includes constitutions, bills of rights, philosophies of natural human rights (including John Locke), charters about trade, laws of the seas, laws of war, etc.

Implied in the modern condemnation of war and the elaborate structure of just-war ethics, which delineates when war is causally justified (*jus ad bellum*) and what measures are permitted and what are proscribed (*jus in bello*), is a body of human rights that prompts us to prevent war and in humanitarian impulse to intervene and ameliorate the potentials for greater morbidity and mortality that arise in conflict.

In the contemporary cognizance and protection of human rights—what Michael Perry calls the "internationalization of human rights"—is also a broader purpose of acknowledgment and affirmation beyond only the "just rights" of persons vis-à-vis war. The International Bill of Human Rights, which has been ratified by most nations in the world, consists of three documents: the

Theology, Polity, and the Pacific Vision

Universal Declaration of Human Rights (1948); the International Covenant on Civil and Political Rights (1976), and the International Covenant on Economic, Social, and Cultural Rights (1976).

In concord with these three codes exist hundreds of records that affirm the same rights. Perry, a legal philosopher, concludes that these three documents affirm the sacred bearing and being of the human person and as such implicate religion in these conflicts and in their resolution. Once the affirmation of human worth moves along this transcendent level, the notion of human rights as positive law—an evolutionary and therefore arbitrary and relativistic value—is replaced by a deontological or sacred grounding. Now Nietzsche's vehement accusations which became the basis of the aggressive power politics of the modern period are no longer valid. In his vivid way, Perry obliquely draws the inevitable conclusion that a new situation of geopolitics has arrived as a sacred dimension is imputed into international human rights.[5]

In *The Will to Power* Nietzsche writes:

> In moving the doctrine of selflessness and love into the foreground, Christianity was in no way establishing the interests of the species as of higher value than the interests of the individual. Its real *historical* effect, the fateful element in its effect, remains, on the contrary, precisely the enhancement of egoism, of the egoism of the individual, to an extreme (—and to the extreme of individual immortality). Through Christianity, the individual was made so important, so absolute, that he could no longer be sacrificed: but the species endures only through human sacrifice— All "souls" became equal before God: but this is precisely the most dangerous of all possible evaluations! If one regards individuals as equal, one calls the species into question, one encourages a way of life that leads to the ruin of the species: Christianity is the counter-principle to the principle of *selection*. If the degenerate and sick ("the Christian") is to be accorded

---

5. Michael Perry, "Is the Idea of Human Rights Ineliminably Religious?," in *Legal Rights: Historical and Philosophical Perspectives*, eds. Austin Sarat and Thomas R. Kearns (Amherst Series in Law, Jurisprudence, and Social Thought; Ann Arbor: University of Michigan Press, 1996).

Ethics and the Wars of Insurgency

the same value as the healthy ("the pagan") or even more value as in Pascal's judgment concerning sickness and health, then unnaturalness becomes law—

This universal love of man is in practice the preference for the suffering underprivileged degenerate: it has in fact the Lowered and weakened the strength, the responsibility, the lofty duty to sacrifice men. All that remains, according to the Christian scheme of values, is to sacrifice oneself: but this residue of human sacrifice that Christianity concedes and even advises has, from the standpoint of general breeding, no meaning at all. The prosperity of the species is unaffected by the self-sacrifice of this or that individual (—whether it be in the monkish and ascetic manner or, with the aid of crosses, pyres, and scaffolds, as "martyrs" of error). The species requires that the ill-constituted, weak, degenerate, perish: but it was precisely to them that Christianity turned as a conserving force; it further enhance the instinct in the weak, already so powerful, to take care of and preserve themselves and to sustain one another. What is "virtue" and "charity" in Christianity if not just this mutual preservation, this solidarity of the weak, this hampering of selection? What is Christian altruism if not the mass- egoism of the weak, which divines that if all care for one another and each individual will be preserved as long as possible?—

If one does not feel such a disposition as an extreme immorality, as a crime against life, one belongs with the company of the sick and possesses its instincts oneself—

Genuine charity demands sacrifice for the good of the species—it is hard, it is full of self- the overcoming, because it needs human sacrifice. And this pseudo-humaneness called Christianity wants it established that no one should be sacrificed—[6]

The Darwinian principle elucidated by Nietzsche has been the basis of interhuman conflicts and affairs at least in the early modern, post-religious phase of human history. If land was vacant (*terra nullus*) or only scattered with settlements—for example

---

6. Friedrich Nietzsche, *The Will to Power*, trans. Walter Kaufmann and R. J. Hollingdale (New York: Random House, 1968), 141–42.

Theology, Polity, and the Pacific Vision

(North and South Amerindians)—the land must be taken. If another party, tribe, or nation presents itself as weak and vulnerable it must be overtaken or one's own nation is made weak. "Eat or be eaten," Jimmy Hoffa's crude Darwinian formulation which became the early credo of the Teamsters Union, reflects this double necessity. This view also had a divine connotation in the sixteenth and seventeenth centuries of European colonization. For the Spanish Jesuits and the Dutch Calvinists, empty space was rendered vacant by God for subjugation as they called on the texts of Genesis— subdue the earth, take dominion, fill the earth (Gen 1:28—the subject of this author's dissertation). Exploitation is no longer sheer human ambition; it is divine imperative. But now, if indigenous people have rights—if, as Nietzsche decries, the weak, sick, and the vulnerable still have a voice—then the divine and natural right of subjugation has been undermined.

And if, as I argued in *Ethics and the Gulf War*, war itself is fundamentally changing in our time, from destructive to constructive endeavors, and if this development in the history of war is joined to this significant change in the history of values, then a new age of human rights may be ready to begin. The world-historical and spiritual-ethical significance of this change is monumental. We may be changing our view of what we will fight for—what is evil, what is the enemy, what we will use our force and resources to do. We may commit these efforts to healing the sick, feeding the hungry, housing the homeless, and restoring goods as we resist those forces that impede these human goods. If this—however dimly— glimmering hope is on the horizon to provide these ministries of care, it may cast new light on the meaning of the decades-long saga running from Somalia and Haiti to Bosnia and Rwanda.

EXCURSUS: JOHN KERRY, TRIUMPHALISM, AND WOUNDS

Miroslav Volf, one of our eminent theologians in the modern world, hails from Croatia, which makes him painfully aware of the modern agony of Bosnia, Serbia, Srebrenica, and the cache

Ethics and the Wars of Insurgency

of perplexing questions regarding the nature of modern warfare which we have explored. At Yale he works on interfaith issues as these intertwine with the matters of strife and reconciliation under our exploration. His edited volume *A Common Word: Muslims and Christians on Loving God and Neighbor* contains a piece from the new US Secretary of State, John Kerry.

Speaking of his commitment to interfaith engagement, Kerry reflects on his own experience: "We all want to see a great deal of change. Somewhere between religious war and religious harmony is tolerance, acceptance of others freedom to 'A Common Word' for not merely longing for a better dialogue but also standing up and delivering one."[7]

At this point I cannot help but reflect on the irony of two news reports yesterday (April 15, 2013) that shocked the world and showed us how treacherous a world without interfaith peace of which the Secretary of State speaks can be.

1. In an op-ed essay in the *New York Times*, a Yemini prisoner at GITMO, a CIA incarceration center in Cuba, writes, "GITMO is killing me." He had gone on a religious fast (protest hunger strike) after rejecting to what he saw as unjust arrest—now still uncharged after 11 years since 9/11. He was tied down and IV force-fed (remember the Ireland case with the IRA) and was not allowed to pray or read his scriptures (the Qurans were reportedly confiscated and searched).[8]

2. In the second case now emerging, someone or some group planted bombs at the crowded end of the Boston Marathon. Earliest reports speak of a black man, dressed in black with a black backpack (pure evil?) speaking a foreign tongue.[9] And Americans wonder, "Why do they hate us so much?"

---

7. Quoted in *A Common Word: Muslims and Christians on Loving God and Neighbor*, eds. Miroslav Volf, Ghazi bin Muhammad, and Melissa Yarrington (Grand Rapids: Eerdmans, 2010), 200.

8. Samir Naji al Hasan Moqbel, "Gitmo Is Killing Me," *New York Times*, April 15, 2013.

9. "3 Killed, More Than 140 Hurt in Boston Marathon Bombing," *CNN*, This Just In, April 15, 2013, online: http://news.blogs.cnn.com/2013/04/15/

Theology, Polity, and the Pacific Vision

With a more conciliatory tone but still appropriate severe (for American tastes), Kerry reflects triumphantly on his great-grandfather (x8), John Winthrop, founder of the Massachusetts colony and author of the famous Puritan sermon, "The City on the Hill Must Shine around the World—Don't Hide Its Light under a Bushel." Boston—there it is, "The City on the Hill," the mischievous display of American might and colonial hegemony. The celebration now becomes the curse. "Why do they hate us so?" Boston, the Puritan hope of the world. Was this the ambivalent and so misunderstood gift of America to the starving of Somalia? Is this why the tribal gangs shot down Blackhawk?

Kerry now speaks in South Korea. Now two trembling pseudo-triumphalists—one black guy in America and one yellow guy in Korea, both schoolyard basketball junkies—forget their new learned words—"My bad"—and breathe blustering threats to wipe out the other.

Kerry's comments, as always, reflect the politician rectitude: "Our position is very clear. North Korea will not become a nuclear state." We (America) will remain one, along with Russia, China, and others we allow (and build)—e.g., Israel and Pakistan.

And so the new martyrs die and rise—another eight-year-old child in Massachusetts—on "Patriot's Day" no less—and in Mogadishu a child soldier on Frankincense-become-Myrrh Street. And the song returns: "Where have all the flowers gone? Long time passing. . . . Oh, when will they ever learn?"[10]

FORCES TENDING TOWARDS HUMAN RIGHTS

The history of war, as Michael Howard suggests, is irresistibly moving greater and greater precision. In presenting justifying reasons for engaging in conflict, there is greater conviction about the evil to be countermanded and more universal consensus before the cause is joined. The survival of a people and their way of life

---

explosions-near-finish-of-boston-marathon/comment-page-18/.

10. Peter Seeger, "Where Have All the Flowers Gone?" (1955).

Ethics and the Wars of Insurgency

has always been ample motivation for war. But petty personality disputes, shame and disgrace, insignificant boundary controversies, and tyrannical ambitions have never been worthy causes for us to hurt and kill others. Religious difference—even the blasphemous notion of dissing or anathematizing certain others in the erroneous belief that they are discountenanced by God—is the least worthy cause for waging war—maiming or killing other persons.

In his study *Just and Unjust Wars* (1977), Michael Walzer reviews, case by case, the sad chronicle of human-on-human war—especially when those endeavors involve unjust, illegal, and unethical measures. Reviewing the salutary traditions of "justifiable war" and how this heritage elicits a lively and noble body of proscriptions on "unjust war," he has been an outstanding leader in this subject material from his long-standing post at Princeton's Institute of Advanced Study. He found the doctrines and principles of unjust-war theory a sufficient basis to declare the Vietnam War unjust and worthy of sanction. The technological amplification of war weaponry also added for Walzer reasons that this war was insufficiently defensible. First and foremost a philosopher, even though his early historical work was on the Puritans, rational utility and deontological duty made this war harder and harder to justify. Word War II—the campaign to stop Hitler and the Third Reich—and even the Cold War resisting the Communist Bloc were sufficiently cogent and worthy of sacrifice—in contrast to Vietnam. Walzer's military "moral calculus" gave more and more legitimacy to constructive efforts to protect innocent people and to deliver goods for life and well-being

Walzer was reaching, in other words, for legitimate and legitimizing uses of power. Otherwise the theological bottom line was non-violence, helping justice and peace. With all great philosophical minds across the millennia, he was an Augustinian. Walzer's other books that which add to his persuasion on war and peace are *Spheres of Justice* (1983), *Exodus and Revolution* (1985), and *The Jewish Political Tradition* (2 vols., 2000, 2003).

Walzer has prescience into what warfare is becoming in the modern era. We are told today that modern military/security readiness involves precision in interventional action and massive careful humanistic work in preventive endeavor. He knew that effective use of national power in destruction needs to be preceded and followed by rigorous construction.

HUMAN RIGHTS DEFINED

If the only justification for war is to restore peace, then the imperatives of the Universal Declaration of Human Rights will be woven more and more into the security and military policies of nations. The Declaration is based on the US revolutionary charter—"life, liberty, and the pursuit of happiness"—rooted of course in the French Revolution's "Liberté, égalité, fraternité," and behind that in the Puritan and Lockean principles of freedom, resistance to tyranny (bordering on tyrannicide), and the material/spiritual cache of the substance of liberty. Nature and nature's God willed these basic rights for all peoples:

freedom of speech; freedom from fear and want; free and equal dignity for all; life, liberty, and the security of persons; no slavery, arbitrary arrest, detention or exile; fair and public hearing; the right to marriage, family, home, communication, and correspondence; movement and residence within and across borders; right to seek asylum; right to a nation and nationality; security of property; freedom of thought, conscience, expression, religion, assembly, and vote; and work, rest, childcare, education, an adequate standard of living, and retirement security.

The Universal Declaration of Human Rights

Preamble

Whereas recognition of the inherent dignity and of the equal and inalienable rights of all members of the human family is the foundation of freedom, justice and peace in the world,

Ethics and the Wars of Insurgency

Whereas disregard and contempt for human rights have resulted in barbarous acts which have outraged the conscience of mankind, and the advent of a world in which human beings shall enjoy freedom of speech and belief and freedom from fear and want has been proclaimed as the highest aspiration of the common people,

Whereas it is essential, if man is not to be compelled to have recourse, as a last resort, to rebellion against tyranny and oppression, that human rights should be protected by the rule of law,

Whereas it is essential to promote the development of friendly relations between nations,

Whereas the peoples of the United Nations have in the Charter reaffirmed their faith in fundamental human rights, in the dignity and worth of the human person and in the equal rights of men and women and have determined to promote social progress and better standards of life in larger freedom,

Whereas Member States have pledged themselves to achieve, in co-operation with the United Nations, the promotion of universal respect for and observance of human rights and fundamental freedoms,

Whereas a common understanding of these rights and freedoms is of the greatest importance for the full realization of this pledge,

Now, Therefore THE GENERAL ASSEMBLY proclaims THIS UNIVERSAL DECLARATION OF HUMAN RIGHTS as a common standard of achievement for all peoples and all nations, to the end that every individual and every organ of society, keeping this Declaration constantly in mind, shall strive by teaching and education to promote respect for these rights and freedoms and by progressive measures, national and international, to secure their universal and effective recognition and observance, both among the peoples of Member States themselves and among the peoples of territories under their jurisdiction.

Article 1.
All human beings are born free and equal in dignity and rights. They are endowed with reason and conscience and should act towards one another in a spirit of brotherhood.

Article 2.
Everyone is entitled to all the rights and freedoms set forth in this Declaration, without distinction of any kind, such as race, colour, sex, language, religion, political or other opinion, national or social origin, property, birth or other status. Furthermore, no distinction shall be made on the basis of the political, jurisdictional or international status of the country or territory to which a person belongs, whether it be independent, trust, non-self-governing or under any other limitation of sovereignty.

Article 3.
Everyone has the right to life, liberty and security of person.

Article 4.
No one shall be held in slavery or servitude; slavery and the slave trade shall be prohibited in all their forms.

Article 5.
No one shall be subjected to torture or to cruel, inhuman or degrading treatment or punishment.

Article 6.
Everyone has the right to recognition everywhere as a person before the law.

Article 7.
All are equal before the law and are entitled without any discrimination to equal protection of the law. All are entitled to equal protection against any discrimination in

violation of this Declaration and against any incitement to such discrimination.

Article 8.
Everyone has the right to an effective remedy by the competent national tribunals for acts violating the fundamental rights granted him by the constitution or by law.

Article 9.
No one shall be subjected to arbitrary arrest, detention or exile.

Article 10.
Everyone is entitled in full equality to a fair and public hearing by an independent and impartial tribunal, in the determination of his rights and obligations and of any criminal charge against him.

Article 11.
(1) Everyone charged with a penal offence has the right to be presumed innocent until proved guilty according to law in a public trial at which he has had all the guarantees necessary for his defence.

(2) No one shall be held guilty of any penal offence on account of any act or omission which did not constitute a penal offence, under national or international law, at the time when it was committed. Nor shall a heavier penalty be imposed than the one that was applicable at the time the penal offence was committed.

Article 12.
No one shall be subjected to arbitrary interference with his privacy, family, home or correspondence, nor to attacks upon his honour and reputation. Everyone has the right to the protection of the law against such interference or attacks.

Article 13.

(1) Everyone has the right to freedom of movement and residence within the borders of each state.

(2) Everyone has the right to leave any country, including his own, and to return to his country.

Article 14.
(1) Everyone has the right to seek and to enjoy in other countries asylum from persecution.

(2) This right may not be invoked in the case of prosecutions genuinely arising from non-political crimes or from acts contrary to the purposes and principles of the United Nations.

Article 15.
(1) Everyone has the right to a nationality.

(2) No one shall be arbitrarily deprived of his nationality nor denied the right to change his nationality.

Article 16.
(1) Men and women of full age, without any limitation due to race, nationality or religion, have the right to marry and to found a family. They are entitled to equal rights as to marriage, during marriage and at its dissolution.

(2) Marriage shall be entered into only with the free and full consent of the intending spouses.

(3) The family is the natural and fundamental group unit of society and is entitled to protection by society and the State.

Article 17.
(1) Everyone has the right to own property alone as well as in association with others.

(2) No one shall be arbitrarily deprived of his property.

Article 18.
Everyone has the right to freedom of thought, conscience and religion; this right includes freedom to change his

religion or belief, and freedom, either alone or in community with others and in public or private, to manifest his religion or belief in teaching, practice, worship and observance.

Article 19.

Everyone has the right to freedom of opinion and expression; this right includes freedom to hold opinions without interference and to seek, receive and impart information and ideas through any media and regardless of frontiers.

Article 20.

(1) Everyone has the right to freedom of peaceful assembly and association.

(2) No one may be compelled to belong to an association.

Article 21.

(1) Everyone has the right to take part in the government of his country, directly or through freely chosen representatives.

(2) Everyone has the right of equal access to public service in his country.

(3) The will of the people shall be the basis of the authority of government; this will shall be expressed in periodic and genuine elections which shall be by universal and equal suffrage and shall be held by secret vote or by equivalent free voting procedures.

Article 22.

Everyone, as a member of society, has the right to social security and is entitled to realization, through national effort and international co-operation and in accordance with the organization and resources of each State, of the economic, social and cultural rights indispensable for his dignity and the free development of his personality.

Article 23.
(1) Everyone has the right to work, to free choice of employment, to just and favourable conditions of work and to protection against unemployment.

(2) Everyone, without any discrimination, has the right to equal pay for equal work.

(3) Everyone who works has the right to just and favourable remuneration ensuring for himself and his family an existence worthy of human dignity, and supplemented, if necessary, by other means of social protection.

(4) Everyone has the right to form and to join trade unions for the protection of his interests.

Article 24.
Everyone has the right to rest and leisure, including reasonable limitation of working hours and periodic holidays with pay.

Article 25.
(1) Everyone has the right to a standard of living adequate for the health and well-being of himself and of his family, including food, clothing, housing and medical care and necessary social services, and the right to security in the event of unemployment, sickness, disability, widowhood, old age or other lack of livelihood in circumstances beyond his control.

(2) Motherhood and childhood are entitled to special care and assistance. All children, whether born in or out of wedlock, shall enjoy the same social protection.

Article 26.
(1) Everyone has the right to education. Education shall be free, at least in the elementary and fundamental stages. Elementary education shall be compulsory. Technical and professional education shall be made generally available and higher education shall be equally accessible to all on the basis of merit.

(2) Education shall be directed to the full development of the human personality and to the strengthening of respect for human rights and fundamental freedoms. It shall promote understanding, tolerance and friendship among all nations, racial or religious groups, and shall further the activities of the United Nations for the maintenance of peace.

(3) Parents have a prior right to choose the kind of education that shall be given to their children.

Article 27.

(1) Everyone has the right freely to participate in the cultural life of the community, to enjoy the arts and to share in scientific advancement and its benefits.

(2) Everyone has the right to the protection of the moral and material interests resulting from any scientific, literary or artistic production of which he is the author.

Article 28.

Everyone is entitled to a social and international order in which the rights and freedoms set forth in this Declaration can be fully realized.

Article 29.

(1) Everyone has duties to the community in which alone the free and full development of his personality is possible.

(2) In the exercise of his rights and freedoms, everyone shall be subject only to such limitations as are determined by law solely for the purpose of securing due recognition and respect for the rights and freedoms of others and of meeting the just requirements of morality, public order and the general welfare in a democratic society.

(3) These rights and freedoms may in no case be exercised contrary to the purposes and principles of the United Nations.

Theology, Polity, and the Pacific Vision

Article 30.
Nothing in this Declaration may be interpreted as implying for any State, group or person any right to engage in any activity or to perform any act aimed at the destruction of any of the rights and freedoms set forth herein.[11]

COMMENTARY

Part of the vagueness of the present discussion comes with the high idealism of these universal documents. Like the WHO's definition of health—" . . . not merely the absence of disease but the presence of physical, mental and social well-being"—these universal idealistic documents are inclined toward excess of generality, comprehensiveness, and impracticality—in general, a lack of realism in what they promise and can provide.

The roster of formal negative rights are perhaps easier to defend and supply. No one has to give you anything for the freedom of speech, assembly, press, religion, travel, etc. but the substantive positive rights require that something be given—work, food, shelter, healthcare, education, etc. In the casuistic debates now going on between China and the United States, for example, we call for an end to arrest for political dissent and for free speech, freedom to immigrate and travel, free markets, etc. At the same time, China condemns our handgun violence, drug abuse, and corruption in business and politics while they extol their record of securing real " tangible rights"—work, food, shelter, healthcare, and education.

As we will see, as our argument unfolds both senses of human rights—formal and substantive—are embedded in the Judaic, Hellenic, and Christian traditions. Both constellations or tablets of rights are noble, worth protecting, and worth fighting for. Indeed, the thesis I will enfold finds the these three dimensions of human rights to be indispensable to a total view and a holistic perspective. Human rights must be grounded in ethical, economical, and eschatological reality. Only in this way can we avoid having only

11. Online: http://www.un.org/en/documents/udhr/.

currency or expediency. The dimensions of historical prophecy, realistic politics, and hopeful prolepsis are fundamental characteristics of human rights.

We will explain these three essential features of human rights and illustrate them with reference to the crises concerning these same rights in places like Somalia, Bosnia, and Rwanda. Human rights is a complex doctrine of what humans are meant to be, what, in fact, in the real world they are, and what they are becoming. The definition of human rights that we will propose is grounded in the meaning of these two words: we must ask what is "human" and what is "right." When we ask what is essential to our humanity, or the "*humanum*," we immediately enter into some kind of normative assertion.

Aristotle saw humans as political animals (members of the *polis*) and persons bearing theological (teleological) potentials—reason, strength, culture, and faith. The realization of the following dimensions and human propensities was held to constitute fulfilled humanness. Biological psychological, social, political, and theological theories have also offered their particular norms. For our purposes we will define human with a mixed-model definition which includes access to the following dimensions of existence:

Biological and physical rudiments of existence: survival, freedom from assault and violence, basic constituents of vitality, family, food, shelter, healthcare, right to live, right to die.

Social provisions for existence: education, cultural life, work, rest and leisure, social security, and provision in seniority.

Qualities of freedom: thought and act, access to literature, press and media, privacy, due process under law, association, travel, speech, faith.

Close scrutiny of these characteristics of fulfilled humanity revealed the necessity of each to any understanding of the human. Without the rudimentary conditions for life there can be no humanness. Humanity is realized in sociality. Without freedom life is not worthy of living. Of course some of these qualities may be lost for a time, be sacrificed for other values or other persons, or be

Theology, Polity, and the Pacific Vision

attenuated in various degrees. Yet when human life is present with some appointment of value (*droit humaine*) something like the above constellation is found. "Right," which we defined not as possession or desire but as basic human need and realization, brings attending obligations both for the subject to seek and claim, and for the society—family, community, government, law—to provide and protect.

The threefold exposition of rights which we follow through this study also bears on our definition. Human rights are rights inherited, actual, and anticipated. They are imperatives given by virtue of our existence from God—natural and inherent, within community and seeking fulfillment and realization in the future. Given by God—received in community (baptism and citizenship)—and here (*Dabei*)—seeking the possibility of actualization (*Dasein*)—open possibility is our claim to and right of life.

This working definition of human rights is rounded out as we review the history and character of the creed and convention of those same human rights. That these rights are intrinsic and inherent in our being human qua human and not earned or contingent in any way is expressed in these paradigmatic texts:

1. God created humanity in God's image (Genesis 1).

2. All persons are endowed by their Creator with certain unalienable rights (US Declaration of Independence).

3. The inherent dignity of all members of the human family (Universal Declaration of Human Rights).

4. These rights derive from the inherent dignity of the human person (International Covenant on Civil and Political Rights).

5. All human rights derive from the dignity and worth inherent in the human person (UN World Congress on Human Rights).

The concept, creed, and convention of human rights emerges in the mid and late twentieth century as a consensus in religion, philosophy, and law has arisen. A long and circuitous road has been traveled as this ethical consensus has emerged against grievous and destructive historical events. Now secular philosophers

Ethics and the Wars of Insurgency

like Daniel Callahan and Ronald Dworkin can join religious philosophers to affirm the sacred, inviolable, value of persons and the formidable rights that rise against this background.

In *Abortion: Law, Choice and Morality* (1973), Callahan affirms the secular version of the sacred value of the human being. Similarly, in Dworkin's *Life's Dominion: An Argument about Abortion, Euthanasia, and Individual Freedom* (1993) he resonates:

> Some readers, I know, will take particular exception to the term "sacred" because it will suggest to them that the conviction I have in mind is necessarily a theistic one. I shall try to explain why it is not, and how it may be, and commonly is, interpreted in a secular as well as conventionally religious way. But "sacred" does have ineliminable religious connotations for many people, and so I will sometimes use "inviolable" instead to mean the same thing, in order to emphasize the availability of that secular interpretation.[12]

The lineage of today's doctrine of human rights and the remarkable synthesis of secular and sacred wisdom has passed through the following the formidable thresholds: the creation of human beings in the *Imago Dei* in freedom and dignity, exposition of the moral law of the universe and of human interrelations, human awakening in the Greco-Roman world, the Jesus revolution of the kingdom of God, the Renaissance and Reformation, the rise of democracy, the philosophical and religious Enlightenment, the citizen revolutions, (US and European), and the modern crisis and insight. As we scan this intellectual and civil history of human rights we will also see how the substance has evolved.

IMAGO DEI

The awakening of human dignity comes around the world by virtue of an awareness to humans that they are fashioned through divine will and spirit in creation and that divine justice shapes their

---

12. Ronald Dworkin, *Life's Dominion: An Argument about Abortion, Euthanasia, and Individual Freedom* (London: HarperCollins, 1993), 251.

Theology, Polity, and the Pacific Vision

very conscience and constitution, framing and constituting their existence in the mirror image of the Divine One so that good and evil are known and discerned and that we are all individually and collectively to bring honor, not harm, to any "other" who we know is also the "friend of God."

In Genesis we have the pivotal articulation of this divine word, will, and way which grounds the creation of all humans—*Imago Dei*. With respect to others we either recognize and work for this inherent dignity or deface and destroy this Image to our own judgment. My teacher in the Protestant faculty of the University of Strasbourg, Jean-François Collange, finds the origination, continuation, and destination (fulfillment) of all human rights in this divine assertion and protection. This school of scholarship where the theology dean eventually moves from the divinity faculty into the presidency of the university, then to mayor of the city, then to the political leadership of the European community, based in Strasbourg, witnesses to the essential continuum of religion to rights in this particular region of the world community and this philosophical formulation of the doctrine.[13]

The Genesis accounts of human origin and human nature concern two matters: divine creation and good intention, and on the other hand human malevolence and violation. The human saga is marked by the high dignity of human being made in love for divine human fellowship and for inter-human love, justice, and peace, and on the other hand the disgrace of what seems to be not only episodic but chronic violence on the part of the sons of Adam and Eve who are genetic criminals—especially Cain, through the killing of Abel. The Genesis document is so frightening that the Lord himself seems arbitrary and his divisive discrimination is ever evident.[14]

Enmity and hatred, plotting, subversion, and murder mark the human condition from its outset. And in the mythic power of Genesis these perversions of the *Imago Dei* are found to be ubiquitous, universal, and perennial. People will always tend toward ruthlessness and only the divine charter can constrain this

---

13. Collange, *Theologie des Droits de L'Homme*.
14. See Jack Miles, *God: A Biography* (New York: Knopf, 1995).

Ethics and the Wars of Insurgency

inherent malevolence and encourage the inherent dignity and equality so that respect and humanity can then shine forth.

Yet the name Yahweh—which is unutterable—will not be defamed. It will be sanctified and not blasphemed by human bloodshed. The divine image will be sustained and the law of "the other" (*l'autre*) will endure.[15] This will become the bedrock foundation of human rights.

Before rushing to that antidote of violence imposed against the world's sickness, we need to document the ubiquity and universality of the malevolence just mentioned. Although, as Reinhold Niebuhr has said, human sin is the most empirically verifiable fact of human nature, many, including some who have contributed mightily to the human rights creed, believe more in the fundamental goodness of humans and attribute the corruption all around to society or even to religion.

Working from Calvin's city of Geneva, Jean Jacques Rousseau along with other figures of French Romanticism and Enlightenment, offer this etiology and analysis. The blight of injustice and inhumanity (*unrecht*) is profoundly with us in the late twentieth century. Sin, as Niebuhr often said, is profound and ubiquitous.

In a way the human rights revolution is a mockery since it is so little implemented and hardly ever enforced. It is so often abrogated and neglected. The primary violence of life today is found in the fact of the inexplicable affluence in some of the world's population and unimaginable misery among the vast majority.

As I gaze from my study window here in Strasbourg, one of the loveliest and most delectable of cities in the world; as I window shop this holiday season and see the cornucopia of chocolates and flowers, clothes and jewelry, foods and autos; as I return to America, the citadel of world power and affluence; I realize why Zaire and Rwanda embarrass and shame us. We have allowed, even in the overdeveloped world, a shameful degradation among the rest.

Calvin thought that the poor among us, those whom we enigmatically and blithely say, "we will always have among us" (Matt

15. Jean-François Collange, *Theologie des Droits de L'Homm* (Paris: Cerf, 1989), 120.

Theology, Polity, and the Pacific Vision

26:11), are a sign to us of the generosity and *gentilesse* of God that we are to mimic so that rich and poor are both dignified. The neglect of the Third World in our midst implies that we have lost not only justice but charity itself.

The foundational character of human rights therefore is indelible because of the character of Yahweh and the historical experience of human malevolence and violence. "You are irrepressibly violent—therefore you must not kill!"

Two charters of ethics emerge in ancient Israel. First there is the universal charter and then the covenantal charter. The universal charter, sometimes called the Noachic law, binds all humanity to a basic series of norms. Viewed in light of the potential for catastrophic malevolence in the human condition and human destruction, an emergency provision (*Notordnungen*) is set down in the earth after the flood, to constrain evil and sustain and maintain the human family on earth. Genesis 9 holds the kernel of an ancient tradition cross-referential to all old Semitic and Near Eastern codification, proscribing killing, torture, abuse of animals, blasphemy, idolatry, adultery, sexual perversion, stealing, and enslavement of humans, while prescribing respect for the natural world and a natural covenant of life with life.[16]

When jurists and military victors (and a few wise men and theologians) contrived after the frightful inhumanity of the Second World War and the Nazi Holocaust to assess guilt and level punishment they appeal to such transnational, universal "Laws of Humanity"—though such, in historical form and actual political reality, never had existed. The particular laws of nations had become suspect since Nazi law had revealed its ethical bankruptcy. "I was only following orders."

The "higher law (biblical) background" of natural-law systems disallowed the practice especially of the legalized crimes against God and humanity sanctioned by the Noachite and

16. See here "Noachitische Gebot," in *Theologische Realenzyklopädie*; Aaron Lichtenstein, *The Seven Laws of Noah* (New York: Jacob Joseph School Press, 1981); A. S. Geyser, "Paul, the Apostolic Decree and the Liberals in Corinth," in *Studia Paulina in Honorem J. de Zwaan*, eds. J. N. Sevenster and W. C. van Unnik (Haarlem: Bohn, 1953), 124-38.

Ethics and the Wars of Insurgency

Decalogic heritage. The practices of blasphemy and murder, sterilization and abortion, became normal practice. Law from the Allied side, however noble, was also always tainted with expediency and self-service.

The "Laws of Humanity" invoked in the two Nuremberg tribunals (the trials of the generals and the doctors) in 1946–1947 and the "Statutes" (war crimes, etc.) in 1947–1948, along with the derivative UN Declaration of Human Rights, all appeal to a somewhat vague, idealistic, ironically Talmudic and Judaic, yet powerfully transcendent and humanistic standard.

Andrew Ivy, the physician at my medical school (the University of Illinois), a pietistic Methodist layperson from Oak Park, Illinois, who represented American medicine at the trials (he also drafted the Nuremberg Code of Medical Ethics), appealed to Wesleyan perfectionism grounded in the Sermon on the Mount as well as other bedrocks of ethics, such as the Hammurabic Code, the Oath of Hippocrates, and other such salient documents, creating a strange yet sublime mélange and admixture of sacred and secular idiom which has endured in legal, political, and medical practice to this day. It has exhibited a lively currency and relevance, creating the ground doctrine of human rights for all time.

Behind and alongside biblical ethics is a general heritage—philosophical and humanistic—which flows into the great river we call the human rights tradition. This coalition of sacred and secular power was necessary to combat the fratricidal, genocidal, ecocidal—yea, even deicidal—furies of the twentieth century.

Princeton's Max Stackhouse therefore grounds the human rights tradition in Hebrew pan-religious impulses, the high prophets of the Abrahamic faiths all mediated through the exilic priests who synthesized and appropriated this composite heritage to world-historical crises. The themes Stackhouse finds relevant are: the reality of God as "Other" and the grounding inter-human concern for the "other." All humans stand under the ultimate reality and justice of God, whether we know and acknowledge that "one God" or not. We also stand accountable to human and secular law, which is the will of that "great God" for all societies and all

Theology, Polity, and the Pacific Vision

religions. Even post-religious culture must assert this higher law without which "human rights" is so easily abrogated.

Only with the "one God" of creation and redemption inscribed can the questions "Am I my brother's keeper?" and "Who is my neighbor?" be fully addressed. These architectonic and metaethical questions beg the God question since loving one's neighbor may involve "laying down one's life." Conversely, the God matter implies the human. As G. F. Handel exclaims at the end of the *Messiah*, following the Apostle Paul in 1 Corinthians 15:21, "For since by man came death, by man came also the resurrection of the dead." The whole God thing is inextricably woven into the human. With the coming of the age of human rights, the human and the divine question become inextricable.

The divine encounter-engagement with Israel also produced a particular and parochial covenant along with its universal import. The Decalogue and its enfolding Torah became the ethical charter of the prophets, who transformed political history, making it the craft of God's justice and of the Jesus movement and Christianity through the Sermon on the Mount. From Sinai and Beatitudes Mountain would come a wisdom so precious and demanding that it would convey "glory to my people Israel" and "a light to the Gentiles." This illuminating wisdom and law would eventually ground human rights along with the necessary respect, will to protect this right in others, and efforts to implement these same principles.

HUMAN RIGHTS IN GRECO-ROMAN CULTURE

Greece and Rome elevated the rights of citizens to new heights. Granted, these rights were not extended to foreigners, slaves, women, or even the poor (non-landowners), yet these cultures achieved a breakthrough in political philosophy and practical politics that was to provide another plank in the platform for a modern agenda of human rights. Plato, Aristotle, and the Stoics achieved ethical insights that would mark Mediterranean-Western culture until the sixth century, then to disappear with the loss of Greek consciousness from the Holy Roman Empire only to be recovered with the

Arabic, Islamic renaissance of Greek learning in the southern edges of Europe in the eleventh century. This would, in turn, exert great influence on the European Renaissance.

The Greeks believed that a world of idea ideas and ideals was the most real realm of reality. These ideals extended to the nature of the human being, freedom, purpose, and virtue. The good for Socrates, Plato, and then Aristotle is to achieve potentials and fulfill inherent propensities (*teloi*). Humans are imbued with souls—animal at one level, but rational and spiritual at the epitome. Fulfillment required the exercise of these higher qualities and called for the state through education to train persons in the disciplines of self-realization, recognition, and respect of the quest for rights in others. While the nobility of the human person—the soulful and glorious freedom that reason bestows—is extolled, there is also a hierarchism, an arrogance and elitism that penetrates Greek consciousness. As we noted earlier with reference to Nietzsche, a contempt for the week, vulnerable, and voiceless accompanies the Greek view of human fulfillment (sound mind in the beautiful body) and the view of excellence in human achievement.

Christian concerns for the marginalized and, in Jesus and Paul, the affirmation of the foolish and weak of the world, were offensive to Greek anthropology. Yet the lasting contribution of Greece and Rome to our theme is that citizenship conveys nobility and protection. Arbitrary will and power are now chastened by the realm of law. The apostle Paul appeals to his rights as a Roman citizen when local antagonism would have killed or exiled him.

HUMAN RIGHTS IN CHRISTIAN PERSPECTIVE

When earth-citizenship was joined in Christian culture to the heavenly citizenship of baptism, a formidable estimate of human value is born. Human rights in Christian perspective require that at this point we must note the importance of the Jesus movement and Christian faith in the evolution of human rights. On the one hand there is a diminution of purely secular values regarding the human both in spirituality of Christianity and in its suspicion about human goodness and achievement. Yet the profound and overarching impact of Christianity on human rights is to affirm the intrinsic God-given dignity and worth of all persons. The emphasis on the rights of heretofore dispossessed persons—women, children, the poor, and strangers (aliens, immigrants)—is strong in Christianity. Though citizenship is eschatological and worldly rights and goods are deemphasized, the secular impact of the faith on establishing kingdoms and the cities of law, rights, and righteousness is a mark of Christian history.

Jesus not only affirmed but deepened the Mosaic Law in the Sermon on the Mount, perhaps the greatest Christian religious text on human rights. In passages such as "not one jot or tittle shall in no wise pass from the law"(Matt 5:18), the divine ground of human right, respect, and dignity is firmly placed in the day-to-day affairs of people. Political authority is affirmed by Paul as an instrumentality of divine regulation and humanization of our common life. As Christian world history would prove, civic leaders were held to these responsibilities before God even over against the church. The protection and affirmation of human rights and goods was the justification for government. If these obligations were neglected, that government was invalidated.

Collange, a New Testament scholar, structures much of his rationale for a human rights project and process in the Christian Scriptures. The background of his book *Theologie des Droits de l'Homme* is grounded in the word of creation and of incarnation. Collange's reading of the biblical faith firmly positions human rights and correlative duties not in heaven but on earth. The cardinal doctrines of creation and incarnation ground the creed here not there. The crisis of Cain and Abel, for example, where one cries out against violence—God hears and answers—and this then leads to law as God's word establishes justice and human law—the human retort "so help me God"—confirms that divine word.

From the Christian Testament Collange builds his argument around Jesus' enigmatic teaching about kingdom and authority in the Gospels. Here we are taught to submit to Caesar's authority in its proper place and to retain for God his rightful Lordship (Mark

Ethics and the Wars of Insurgency

12:17). Christ's kingdom, the realm of ultimate salvation and righteousness, is not of this world (John 18:36.) Then, in perhaps the Gospels' most enigmatic teaching on *exousia* (power, authority), Jesus says in John 19:11 to Pilate concerning his incarceration and death sentence "You would have no power over me if it were not given to you from above."

Perplexing questions arise. Was Jesus' execution authorized by God? Was this infamous abrogation of rights and justice some kind of acquiescence to worldly authority even when it was unjust and in the wrong? Paul, in Romans 13, where he pleas for obedience to worldly authority, seems to concur with Jesus' message to the zealots not to take politics into their own hands and seek to overthrow earthly established authority. Jesus seemed to anticipate the violent eradication of the Jewish state, fragile as it was, in the Jewish-Roman War of 66–70 CE. Pacific and nonviolent resistance even to demonic authority is one possible reading of Jesus' human rights ethic. What is Jesus' life and teaching about? What does his death, resurrection, and continuing session and intercession mean? What significance does Jesus have for our theme of human rights? Let us list some of the meanings:

1. Jesus teaches the kingdom of God. In this realm and reign people are healed, cleansed, and made right within themselves, with others, and with God. Jesus' own response to people—even sinners, the sick and infectious, the despised, outcasts and children—was respect and love.

2. He condemned presumption before God and disdain toward people. He thus extolled a human-to-human norm—"Love one another" (John 13:34).

3. He gave us a new kind of society where love, not hate or jealousy, prevailed. He exemplified the coming realm into this realm and taught us to believe in it and live to bring it about. In associating our lives with his, he still lives and is with us as we overcome fears and sickness, living as if on our own, abandonment and alienation from God, and ways of life where other people are exploited, harmed, and disrespected.

Theology, Polity, and the Pacific Vision

Living with and toward Jesus, with ourselves, in our homes, in our churches, communities, cities, nations, and world, we fashion a new kind of world where people matter and where respect, justice, reconciliation, and peace continually challenge and displace the worldly way of taking advantage of, stepping on, wounding, and ignoring others.

4. Where possible we inform politics, policies, social structures, laws, and public processes with these principles. We always seek to transform this still harsh and still mean economy with God's economy (Athanasius).

5. Christian ethics seeks to live in the vast network of our associations in the imitation of God as known in Jesus Christ. What we have seen of God in the face of Jesus is a God of love, justice, forgiveness, and peace. We seek to show this face into the world. In his cross, resurrection, ascension and session, ever-presence and impending return, Jesus sets the world which God so loved in a new course.

Jesus' coming to the world leads us to believe that in him God has initiated a project of remaking and restoring the world into what it was meant to be. In this "becoming world" God's law will find adherents and delight. Peace will displace war and "They shall not hurt nor destroy in all my holy mountain: for the earth shall be full of the knowledge of the Lord, as the waters cover the sea" (Isa 11:9).

What has this reflection on Jesus to do with the concept and concourse of human rights? At the simplest level, those who interpret reality in theo-christocentric ways appropriate the preceding insights into their political commitments.

When we elected Woodrow Wilson as president of the United States we mandated his nascent ideas about a League of Nations. When we elected Harry Truman an then Dwight Eisenhower we expected them to confirm human rights commitments in the post-war European theater. When we elected and reelected Bill Clinton we hoped that he would pursue the now codified human rights principles in our doings with China, Rwanda, Israel, and Bosnia,

Ethics and the Wars of Insurgency

as well as in unforeseen developments in geopolitics. We expect an Obama regime to be constitutionally driven and justice derived—like Dr. King's "beloved community."

At another level we seek through ecumenical dialogue a convergence of commitment to human rights: in local and international dialogue with Jews, Muslims, Buddhists, and Hindus. We seek common pathways toward human rights based on the considerable body of common faith and tradition. A third level of relevance is one we have attempted in the work of our Center for Ethics and Values at Garrett Seminary in the program path on "War and Peace."

Bosnia serves as the best example because of our ability to involve the three communities—Serbian Orthodox, Croatian Catholic, and Bosnian Muslim—as they are broadly represented in Chicago. Since we have already cited this example let me illustrate this point with our project on Armenia and Turkey.

What we seek to do in this project is work through religious channels to bring ethical issues of strife into focus, determine pathways of justice, human rights, and reconciliation, and then finally influence local, national, and international policy—as we are able. After initial planning sessions with the involved communities—Armenian Orthodox and even the Islamic Turks—we bring together the expert historians, theologians, and ethicists to examine issues such as genocide, Islamic jihad in Eastern Anatolia, and Armenian partisanship with Russian war efforts against the Ottoman Empire of Islam in Eastern Europe and in the western Near East.

We also look at the imperialism of the Armenian national church as we search out what makes for strife and peace. Through roundtable processing of the insights developed, we seek to influence American, Armenian, and Turkish policy with the values and established principles that have been identified, among these being human rights, justice, and freedom. At this point Christians or Jews and Muslims seek to find a secular nomenclature and pluralistic consensus for their faith-derived values and beliefs. The cultural activities of philosophy, political science, and other

Theology, Polity, and the Pacific Vision

secular disciplines then are appropriated into a final version of Christian witness within a secular pluralistic ethos. This blended approach allows for the church to be the church and the state to be the state—both authentically modeling a new humanity. This presents a norm to set over against an expediency ethic which otherwise is customary.

John Howard Yoder in his book *The Original Revolution* puts it this way:

> ... the ultimate and most profound reason to consider Christ—rather than democracy or justice, or equality or liberty—as the hope of the world, is not the negative observation, clear enough already, that hopes of this kind generally remain incomplete and disappointing, or that they can lead those who trust them to pride or brutality. The fundamental limitation of these hopes is found in the fact that in their search for power and in the urgency with which they seek to guarantee justice they are still not powerful enough. They locate the greatest need of man in the wrong place. Those for whom Jesus Christ is the hope of the world will for this reason not measure their contemporary social involvement by its efficacy for tomorrow nor by its success in providing work, or freedom in all, or food or in building a new social structures, but in identifying with the Lord in whom they have placed their trust.[17]

THE HISTORICAL LEGACY OF CHRISTIAN "RIGHTS"

More normative to Christian belief and Jesus' teaching is the mandate to responsible citizenship. Here the state is called to the perception and protection of human values. Politics is the realm of justice where human goods and rights are promulgated and protected. Christian history, especially Constantinian, Justinian,

---

17. John Howard Yoder, *The Original Revolution: Essays on Christian Pacifism* (Scottdale, PA: Herald, 1972), 165–66.

Ethics and the Wars of Insurgency

Wycliffian, and Reformed doctrine more generally, displays this notion of human rights. The church as God's family now transcends earthly families, tribes, and nations, and the ground of the universal brotherhood of the human family is established.

In the Middle Ages the recovery of Greek wisdom through the Arab sojourners in Spain and Italy was joined to Christian insight in thinkers like Thomas Aquinas to create a doctrine of human rights grounded in reason and faith. The great generation of theorists of such rights—Nicholas of Cusa, John Wycliffe, Jan Hus, Suarez, Grotius and others—would shape these theological foundations into an agenda of practical politics.

In documents such as the Magna Carta of England (1215) Wycliffe's *De Civili Dominio* (1380) and Luther's "Concerning Christian Liberty" and "Letter to the Christian Nobility (1520) we find this heritage of thought. Book 22 in Calvin's *Institutes of the Christian Religion* (1538), in particular, is a foundation where the "rights of man" is being built. Calvin and the Puritans are critical to this emergence. Max Stackhouse argues that the pivotal epoch in this development comes with the Calvinists and Puritans of the sixteenth century in France and Switzerland and the next generations of Puritans and Calvinists in England, Holland, and America. Additionally he contends that evangelical Calvinism such as is found among the Puritans and Reformation conservatives ironically is not conducive to human rights: ". . . this type of Calvinism sees the radical corruption of the fall so profoundly that claims about human rights border on arrogant pride."[18]

While agreeing with Stackhouse's position on human rights in the Calvinist ethos, I disagree with him at this point. It seems to me that this anthropology of suspicion—the doctrine of the profound fall in Calvin and in his evangelical and pietistic followers—is in fact the strongest source of human rights theory. That humans cannot be trusted to respect, do justice, and be concerned for the goods and freedoms of other persons is the very reason we need the "separation of powers" and "checks and balances."

---

18. Max L. Stackhouse, *Creeds, Society, and Human Rights: A Study in Three Cultures* (Grand Rapids: Eerdmans, 1984), 58.

Theology, Polity, and the Pacific Vision

Viable political organization, democratic processes, and constitutional safeguarding of human rights flow from this estimation of human goodness. It is Calvin's pessimism regarding human nature that forms a strong building block of rights theory, and the ground of rights theory here is not the innate worth of human beings but the hedging and checking of human abuse. Humans are the "glory of God," but in their subservience to deity and their justice lived in the Spirit. It is no accident that a good portion of legal professionals in America are Jews and Calvinists.

It is in his third use of the law, not the second (constraint of evil), that Stackhouse finds the impulse for human rights legislation in Calvin's work. Here the law of God serves as a sanctified force in human life creating the condition for human betterment, justice, and fulfillment of the imperative to encourage persons, however depraved, to proceed in faith through grace stages of holiness and righteousness. This provides in society the impulses to also create specific programs of healthcare, education, social service, and economic regulation that serve particularly to encourage the meeting those needs and rights in all people. Stackhouse concludes:

> Under God's righteousness, life was governed by a moral law that was severe; it was also, by God's grace, dynamic and liberating. Individual rights were given a firm foundation—indeed, a divine foundation—in the membership of God's Humanum.[19]

In the political consciousness of three faith communities derivative of the broader Calvinist ethos—evangelicals, imperialists, and "free church" voluntarists—these very convictions begin to work themselves out in the social order.

THE ENLIGHTENMENT

Historians claim that the Calvinist revolution in Europe provided the seedbed for the democratic and human rights revolution that we associate with Puritan England, the founding of America, and

19. Ibid., 59.

Ethics and the Wars of Insurgency

developments in France, Holland, Switzerland, and elsewhere in seventeenth- and eighteenth-century Europe. This perspective is associated with names like Voltaire (*Traité sur la Tolérance*, 1763), Rousseau, and Montesquieu in France. In England, Locke's father was a Puritan divine though his own thought was more secular. He was thrown into a conservative position on the natural moral law—a fundamental Puritan assertion—by virtue of being spokesman against Hobbes's anarchism. For Locke, values such as life, freedom, and property are self-evident, not only to faith but to reason, as they are verified in experience. Locke's influence on democratic movements in Europe, and especially on the American Revolution, Bill of Rights, and Constitution, is evident. The American experiment in democracy would not only intrigue the world with this bold idea but would identify the role of that government to maintain at home and missionize the world with democracy grounded in human rights. Indeed human rights and participatory freedom-based government are part of the theological substance of the Puritan faith. After the final death gasp of European imperialism and totalitarianism in the Third Reich, this residual ethos remains even stronger until the expediency ethics of recent times.

Having now sketched a brief theological history of human rights doctrine, the task remains to justify this approach in my own analysis and then offer a framework for interpreting the contemporary challenges to human rights commitments. The most compelling recent argument for a theological-ethical grounding for human rights is found in the significant work of Michael Perry.

A RECENT SYNTHESIS EVALUATED

Perry is a law professor at Northwestern University in Chicago. He has found a correlation and synergy between theological belief and action (faith and life) very similar to the one we have just traced with reference to the work of Max Stackhouse. My own normative framework adds to Perry's contributions to jurisprudence a biblical-theological structure that I hope will appeal to persons and nations in the family of Abrahamic faiths as well as the Buddhist,

Theology, Polity, and the Pacific Vision

Hindu, and secular-humanist traditions. Before offering what might be called a prophetic, political, and pastoral framework to analyze the cache of contemporary humanitarian and human rights crises represented by Rwanda, Bosnia, and Somalia, let me add a footnote to Perry's argument.

Though America is the world's most direct heir of the Calvinist-Puritan rights heritage and the most influential purveyor of that tradition into the modern world, our commitments have not been notable. Still shocked by the shambles of Somalia, the failed war in Vietnam, and the clouded glory of the Second World War—disgraced at the outset by the failure in America to accept Jewish refugees from Europe or act on the early data about the Holocaust, and at the end by the genocidal and unjust war tactics of Hiroshima and the incendiary bombing of civilian populations in the German cities—America has not enjoyed the ethical credibility to spearhead human rights in the world. This discredit is complicated by a very shallow concern for human rights in the Reagan, Bush, and Clinton administrations. As two pieces of evidence for this equivocation I include a passage from Jerome Shestack in the *Harvard Human Rights Yearbook* and one from from an opinion letter in the *New York Times* by editor A. M. Rosenthal:

> With determined concentration, President Clinton has worked a historic change in American foreign policy. Foreign policy amounts to a nation's political, moral and military stance in the world, its role and values. For America, the change will affect all these, and for ill. Mr. Clinton has made trade the foundation of his foreign policy, far surpassing other traditional American goals and values, like democracy and human rights, and often overriding security interests. Central to this change is China, with whose President he has decided to exchange state visits, to further his suddenly proclaimed "partnership" between the world's largest democracy and its largest tyranny. The message he sent to all who hoped the U.S. would help them attain some relief from political oppression and religious persecution is: Don't.[20]

20. A. M. Rosenthal, "Bill Clinton's New America," *New York Times*,

Ethics and the Wars of Insurgency

> What reasons should motivate an administration to afford human rights a central role in the United States foreign policy as a matter of national interest?[21]

Here is my response: I believe that there are at least the following compelling motivations to maintain the connection of theological righteousness and human rights doctrine and concrete political action:

1. Human rights values advance national security. Nations that accept human rights are more likely to be stable and make better allies. Repression of human rights invites interventions and endangered stability. Conversely, human rights' responsiveness to the will of the people and restraints on aggressive action foster peace and security.

2. Human rights and world peace are interrelated. Peace and stability cannot be maintained in a world in which people are repressed and impelled to rise up against their oppressors. Afghanistan, Armenia, the Philippines and many other places in the world are stark examples.

3. Human rights are premised on the observation of rules of international law. Acceptance of the rule of law is a condition for a system of world order, which in turn promotes world peace.

4. Human rights have become an essential item on the global agenda, appealing to the expectations of people on every continent. The United States is perceived as having an immense potential to further human dignity and freedom. Championing human rights affords the US the opportunity to be relevant to that agenda and responsive to the aspiration of peoples around the world.

Opinion, November 26, 1996.

21. Jerome Shestack, "An Unsteady Focus: The Vulnerabilities of the Reagan Administration's Human Rights Policy," *Harvard Human Rights Yearbook* 2 (Spring 1989), 25.

Theology, Polity, and the Pacific Vision

5. Advancing economic and social human rights removes causes of tension and inability instability among less developed nations and promotes an equitable world order.

6. Human rights endeavors offer the United States the opportunity to act in concert with other nations to generate "coalitions of shared purposes."

7. Human rights addresses one of the world's most pressing problems: the enormous increase of refugees. The plight of refugees contributes to international tensions, and refugees impose huge burdens on the nations to which they flee. Enforcing human rights will alleviate the suffering and number of refugees.

8. Including human rights in foreign policy formulation is favored by Congress. Without accommodation to this concern the executive branch faces a polarized foreign policy marked by continuing disputes with Congress. A consensus with Congress on human rights issues advances the effectiveness and reliability of United States foreign policy initiatives.

9. Human rights policies command respect and support from this nation's citizenry. Conversely, foreign policies that ignore human rights are likely to be self-defeating by failing to sustain popular support.

10. Finally, advancing human rights reinforces this nation's own cohesion, it's moral purpose, and its appreciation of its own domestic liberties. Human rights have long been a focus for shared purpose in this nation's tradition, and a sense of shared purpose among its people is in the national interest.

AMERICA AND THE HERITAGE OF HUMAN RIGHTS

Despite these serious regressions in American commitment to human rights and her advocacy of these standards into world history, it remains the fact that we are responsible for introducing much of

Ethics and the Wars of Insurgency

the substance of modern human rights theory and remain active in its implementation. Three reasons undergird this responsibility:

- America is the principal purveyor of the Calvinist-Puritan-Lockean and democratic spirit of human rights in world history.

- America gave voice to the early codification of human rights doctrine through its leadership in the post-World War II conventions: the United Nations, Nuremberg trials, etc.

- America now has unequaled and unprecedented power and influence in world affairs. "For unto whomsoever much is given, of him shall be much required" (Luke 12:48).

Even North Vietnam's war for independence was fashioned on the basis of America's declaration, Constitution, and Bill of Rights. The irony of American planes bombing this small country to smithereens was doubly pronounced given this fact.

In the philosophy and ethics of history that undergirds this essay, and my own theological approach to political issues, the moral burden placed on particular nations at particular times is great and godly. Cyrus the Persian is Yahweh's shepherd at a critical moment in world history (Isa 44:28). At the axis point of history, Jesus the Christ appears and speaks of Pilate's trusteeship in the Roman Empire in the early first century CE. "Thou couldest have no power at all against me, except it were given thee from above" (John 19:11).

And even now as the Christian presence in the world begins to unfold with the Gentile mission of Paul, we read: "today in accord with eternal command of God the ministry kept secret for long ages is now disclosed to the Gentiles through the prophetic writings" (Rom 16:25–26, paraphrase).

Nations have particular and peculiar destinies in human history and in the history of salvation (Acts 17:26). These destinies and responsibilities come from the gifts and powers imbued in these nations, just as individual accountability rises from gifts possessed by those persons.

Theology, Polity, and the Pacific Vision

The particular moral destiny once reserved to Israel then to the Western Christian empire, then to Puritan America, now is the heritage of all nations (*ethne*)—the universal Gentile mission. The concourse of the gospel to "the ends of the earth" is now accomplished as is the Genesis mandate to "fill the earth and subdue it" (Gen 1:28 NIV). Now the world is being called to become a community of nations within a universal history. Part of this universal history and *Heilsgeschichte* ("sacred history") is the codification of universal human and humanitarian rights. In my reading of theological history this impetus comes from the Torah and Decalogue as the universal laws of human righteousness are conveyed through the history of Israel. This history of meaning and ethics is further conveyed along with the derivative histories of Christianity, modern Judaism, and Islam.

Israel brought divine judgment on itself by reason of its demand for worldly power and materialistic prosperity. Similarly, the Christian church wrongfully sought earthly power and in the process denied its rootage in Mosaic and prophetic Judaism. In its complicity with anti-Semitism, culminating in the European Holocaust, the church has brought God's judgment on itself and on its constituent nations.

Today it is the oppressed peoples of the world who cry out for their human rights. These peoples are the avant-garde of divine and human history as the breaking kingdom of justice is being restored in the world.

America, for a brief moment of history, has carried the burden of being the new Israel for world history. Now in her arrogance, hunger for military power, and material wealth and her negation of God, she may have forfeited her divine destiny and given it over to those dispossessed peoples of the earth both within the Western (Judeo-Christian) commonwealth and without.

The universal saga of nations today is related to the arousal of aspiration of the peoples of Africa, the concourse of Islam on that continent and elsewhere, e.g., Bosnia and Turkey and other phenomenon. In 2013 the European community held out the hope for membership in the Union if Serbia and Kosovo would sign a

Ethics and the Wars of Insurgency

covenant ending civil and religious strife and declaring a commitment to human rights.

Beyond Africa and the Caucasus, Israel/Palestine remains an epicenter of the global earthquake of terrorism and violation of human rights and life itself. These changes are accompanied by a diminution of the power and influence of America and Europe in the world while China, India, and South America enlarge their influence.

Alongside these dramas of history we see a withdrawal of the influence of Marxism and a rise of the perspectives of liberty and democracy. Both of those parameters of public philosophy will continue to play out in the development of Europe, Eurasia and Russia, Asia, Africa, and Central and South America. Both communism and capitalism have left legacies of justice and equality as well as those of suppression of human rights and degradation of the poor. Meanwhile, the inexorable concourse of the river of the human rights revolution meanders on.

The move to human rights advocacy may be an opportunity for America to reclaim its historic role as the conveyor of human rights under law within the divine economy. If military eminence is obsolete and if Rosenthal's "on target" critique can guide us away from economic idolatry, then human rights advocacy may be America's principal project in the twenty-first century. The current criticism is that there are so many zones of acute need in the world—nearly every nation in Africa, South America, and Southeast Asia (e.g., Bangladesh, etc.)—all needing intervention and massive aid, that it simply overwhelms the collective conscience. Just helping do justice in Africa could totally overwhelm the resources not only of America but of the whole affluent world. The issues of humanitarian aid and humanitarian rights are particularly difficult. Why do we intervene in Bosnia and not the Sudan? Why are human rights lifted up in China, e.g., Tibet, but not in Israel? Does not justice require evenhanded treatment worldwide? The response to be offered from the case we are presenting is that justice requires action, and unless that action is forthcoming

Theology, Polity, and the Pacific Vision

greater misery and greater cost will ensue in the face of divine, natural, and historical judgment.

Bosnia, one of our case studies, is a case in point where the world delayed action for years while genocidal activity was allowed to ensue. Swift and decisive action would have stopped the carnage in its tracks. The notion of evil that we find at the root of biblical faith and which is our ground creed for human rights, is that wrong unpunished only allows wrong to flourish. If suffering caused by human violence and negligence is our requisite task to remedy, if it is human nature to push against boundaries until you are stopped, or test your freedom until it elicits resistance from others, then our laissez-faire negligence has been an encouragement to the violation of human rights.

In Bosnia, America also bears a special responsibility for the human rights project because of its unique role in the modern inception of rights activity. When the Nuremberg conventions laid down the guidelines for war crimes or medical informed consent, American spokespersons like Telford Taylor and Andrew Ivy sought to articulate the human moral vision, which then became encoded in the human rights statutes.

Andrew Ivy, the dean of the medical college where I served for many years, articulated in the Nuremberg Code what he called "the laws of humanity" with reference to medical research and care. At the heart of his doctrine, and at the heart of the Methodist-Calvinist creed he drew on, is the notion of human potential for good and evil. That underlying metaethic which resides in the deeper American and biblical culture that he represents requires that those who make the laws have special responsibility for their implementation.

The third argument is even more self-evident. In a world where two superpowers contend there must be power moves, suasion, and negotiation. With the demise of the former Soviet empire and the rising of the current American empire, responsibility falls more to us, and our moral frailties impede our stepping up to the task. Instead of leadership by example and exertion we are

Ethics and the Wars of Insurgency

hesitant—we are billions of dollars in arrears of our own dues to the UN.

It is true that great power is attenuated in our time. A single terrorist with a bomb can disrupt a whole city or nation. We think of Boston in 2013, along with London, Madrid, New York, and Washington, DC. Conversely, the moral persuasion of one just and good man (Mahatma Gandhi) can bring an empire to its knees in the name of righteousness. Today that power must be exerted in a collegial and respectful manner. This fact should enhance the human rights ethos even more when we have established a cultural and historical line where the heritage of human rights has developed.

We now have to establish responsibility for the continuance of that line. We now need to create from that heritage a framework of values and principles—what in substance we mean by human rights —to provide a matrix of meanings from which we can evaluate three representative crises of human and humanitarian rights: Rwanda, Bosnia, and Somalia. The framework of evaluation I have ordered presents these three case studies in reverse historical sequence so that they will coincide with the crisis that best illustrates that particular value scheme.

I have in mind three layers of ethical perspective that grow out of the human rights tradition we have explored. They can be called the ethical, economic, and eschatological or the prophetic, political, and pastoral. The three levels or layers of meaning reflect the biblical-religious and the philosophical-political traditions of human rights and ethics more generally. They combine the ideal and the practical.

The ethical prophetic dimension of human rights that arose as a result of the human atrocities of the twentieth century has forced us to lay hold on a structure and system of human values or ethics that can be given a normative and universal character. We have searched, in other words, to identify what the philosophical tradition sought in Plato and Aristotle as this contains the ideals or constant universal moral imperatives. Our argument holds that in addition to being rooted in the structures of ideal and noumenal

Theology, Polity, and the Pacific Vision

reality (Plato and Kant) and in human rationality, these values are established in the prophetic word of God. Human justice and rights, in other words, are not only the noblest ethical vision of human imagination; they are grounded in the structure of divine ethical reality itself.

Max Stackhouse presents the essence of the contribution of the Hebrew people to the human rights agenda:

> Whenever the social situation opened up to provide space for the recovery of the central perspectives, prophets rose up to call the Hebrew people once more to their basic perspective and to re-articulate, in view of new and challenging conditions, what the moral law and the expected hope meant. In these Prophets we can see the reaffirmation of covenantal concerns, the ancient creedal foundation of human rights: there is a universal moral order, rooted in the righteousness of God, which is other than ordinary experience yet directly pertinent to ordinary experience; and human responsibility involves action toward the future which can reconcile the contradictions without dissolving the difference between the otherness of God and the human reality. Further, in cities which witnessed the rise of prophets, we find the first glimmerings of a social space from which they were able to oppose false loyalties to both familial-ethnic solidarity and political-economic opportunism. They critiqued efforts to unite ethnicity, covenantal religion, and political power into a single web; they demanded that the people distinguish among them. Nathan critiqued the sexual and military actions of David; Amos attacked the political arrogance of Israel and Judah; Hosea adapted anti-familial images to speak of God's faithfulness added in covenant. The most important natural human associations, familial and political, were placed under a higher law and seen as subject to change in view of the covenantal commitments. A godly future, a truly humane future, depended on it.

In the short run the prophets were not often successful. The loyalties to family and political community obscured the people's

Ethics and the Wars of Insurgency

capacity to read the hints of God and to keep the universal notions of law and hope at the forefront, especially in periods of economic success. In time the society began to crack from within and succumbed to assault from without. On several occasions the people were driven into exile and the Diaspora was placed under the occupation of foreign invaders.

> Ancient Israel was destroyed as an ethnic, theocratic regime. Yet the power of the originating perspective did not collapse under these pressures, even if family institutions and political life were radically altered. The religious-moral dimensions of the tradition were renewed in a fresh way with the creation of Judaism.[22]

The prophetic tradition established an order of human evaluation of the social project and the estimate and treatment of human persons that followed took this basic line:

1. God in creation has established a way of justice, goodness, and peace for the world (*shalom*).

2. This way of life (*Torah*) is made known through law, in Scripture and prophetic speech (reminder and warning).

3. This way of righteousness can be abstracted into general principles—for example, the Golden Rule, the Great Commandment, etc. It can be detailed with exact precision, e.g., the Decalogue or the 614 orthodox commandments.

4. Israeli civil-religious law and Islamic *sharia* follow this pattern today.

5. The righteousness of the "Way of God" can only be enacted in the spirit of love, rescue, and renewal, which is the spirit of God who gives the Way.

6. Human laws, customs, tribunals, social structures, and the like are to embody this way of justice.

---

22. Stackhouse, *Creeds, Society, and Human Rights*, 33–34.

Theology, Polity, and the Pacific Vision

7. When other ways, orders, patterns of human behavior, or moral systems usurp this foundational way they fall under the divine judgment as idolatrous constructs.

Let us consider some of the detail of prophetic human rights ethics. In his epic study *Israel, Its Life and Culture*, Johannes Pederson elaborates into sections the fine-grained detail of what we call prophetic righteousness:

First there is the material on Hebrew common life and its laws: The human person must live in community and partake in reciprocally shared blessing. This harmony or *shalom* is disrupted in the anonymity of large cities.[23] When the love between persons grounded in divine covenant and holiness before God exists, peace and salvation and ensues.[24]

The demand of the weak for assistance activates covenant *shalom*.[25] The good householder, king, governor, or nation, like the Lord, "shall judge the poor" "with righteousness" and "reprove with equity for the meek of the earth" (Isa 11:4). Righteousness is the mutual acknowledgment of persons under and before God.[26]

The avenger has rights of justice but always in the context of law.[27] The law of retaliation is transformed into the good of restitution and renewal.[28] Judges and prophets mediate the divine structure of justice and mercy within human affairs.

Close examination shows that this structure is foundational for our human doctrine of rights, both substantive and procedural. What must be judged must be done in truth and with fairness of process. When justice is resolved, peace is restored. Without justice there is no peace. The subtle transformation of primitive vengeance into a Hammurabic proportionate justice (an eye for an eye) then mutates into the rich justice of recompense, restoration,

---

23. Johannes Pederson, *Israel: Its Life and Culture* (London: Oxford University Press, 1926), 263.
24. Ibid., 311.
25. Ibid., 342.
26. Ibid., 347.
27. Ibid., 393.
28. Ibid., 394.

Ethics and the Wars of Insurgency

forgiveness, and new resolve. This transition from hard justice into the mercy of the heart is evident across the prophetic history of Israel.

Pederson then enumerates the stipulates of the specific historic prophets. We select those stipulates pertaining to human rights—bracketing for clarity the background requirements of cultic purity and divine standing that underlie Hebrew prophetic ethics. This will give us a secular derivative of the sacred literature.

Starting with Samuel in the beginning monarchy, we find the emergence of a new type of prophet—one like Moses who combined prophet, priest, and king—but novel in certain ways. The new prophet is part of a community of "sons of the prophets," who intuits and transmits the spirit of Yahweh—the mediator of the Word (Jer 18:18) who confirms and carries out the mandate of the priestly Torah. Prophets would often bring that word in seasons of calamity and national disaster.

Samuel listens for Yahweh's word in the sanctuary (1 Sam 13), reserving word, wisdom, and power of the three historic Hebraic offices—prophet, priest, and king—to act as judge and settle practical cases (1 Sam 7). The prophet has become the person through whom God carries out his justice and judgments with the people.

Kings often sought to co-opt the prophets but like Nathan they often retained their integrity—refusing to become yes-men, speaking truth and judgment even to King David. The censure often came against the king's lust or lies, his violations of the Torah and the way of Torah.

Elijah also prophesied against Ahab for the seizure of Naboth's vineyard (1 Kgs 21:19ff.). Here the crime was raw, aggressive power used against the possession of another person—an act of theft. In Pederson's words, the prophet's word was mediated in divine action against any breach of the old Israelite law, whether it was a breach of family law or violence and bloodshed, the acquisition of an alien mentality, or devotion by the practice of an alien cult.[29]

---

29. Ibid., 131.

Theology, Polity, and the Pacific Vision

Whether blasphemy and apostasy can in any way be approached, let alone be implemented, by modern and secular law becomes an acute problem in contemporary society, where the vast majority of the world's citizens are theocratic Jews, Christians, Muslims (Sunni or Shiah), Hindus, or Buddhists—often living together within pluralistic states. For the Hebrew prophets secularized society in particular needs intense civic law grounded in the rigors of theocentric ethics.

The prophet mediates Israelite *mishpat*—that command that transcends all particular historical reference, the will of any king, etc. It is an eternal righteousness that is conveyed, and if a prophet's decree lacks concordance with this *mishpat*, he is a false prophet. Amos was neither a prophet or son of a prophet, but a shepherd whom Yahweh made a prophet (Amos 7:12–15).

The prophet conveyed the ancient *shalom* spirit of love and truth. This organic unity of people was the justice and grounded peace of God.

Israel calls the prophet a watchman (Hos 21:11ff.), one who scouts for, oversees, and admonishes people amid danger. In the mid-eighth century Hosea condemns Israel for possessing the Canaanite's land and, in turn, being possessed by their gods (*baalim*). Israel commits adultery against Yahweh; thinking these deities fecund and fertile and that they provided bread, water, flax, oil, and all the provisions of life (Hos 2:4ff.), Israel whores after provision and prosperity spurning the faithful lover, Yahweh. With the betrothal to Yahweh broken, the covenant is ruptured—love and truth are thrown to the wind and violence ensues: swearing falsely, murdering, stealing, lying, and committing adultery proliferate (Hos 4:1ff. and 10:4).

Now, the foreign altars must be thrown down, faithfulness and righteousness restored, and the people are to start again as at the beginning of their history (Hos 11:1). The faithful husband, Yahweh, will then renew the covenant, warfare will be abolished, nature will again not languish but sing for joy, and people will dwell in security, righteousness, and truth (2:17ff.). *Hesed*—the

Ethics and the Wars of Insurgency

trusting and loving fellowship—will then be restored and God will then again fight for, deliver, pacify, and secure his people.

Tsedaka (righteousness) and *mishpat* (justice) shall again pour forth as a mighty river (Amos 5:24). Yahweh, for Amos, is Israel's God but also the God of the neighboring peoples. God has brought forth the Philistine and Aramaean—indeed all peoples are called on to execute Yahweh's judgment. "The Day of the Lord" (Isa 2, Zeph 1, Obad 15, Zech 14) will be a moment of reckoning when evil and dishonor will be exposed and justice will be done in all the world.

The new global law will have to be incumbent upon all those of any faiths and no faith. For now and for the foreseeable future Jews will have to live in Christian and Muslims states, Christians in Islamic states, and Muslims in Christian and Jewish states. Hindus, Buddhists, and Chinese religionists will have to suffer patiently in all of the above places.

In Isaiah the opulent and self-confident of Jerusalem have violated the moral law and enriched themselves by exploiting those whom their mission was to protect: the poor, widows, and orphans (1:23; 5:2; 10:2). These *nouveau riches* do not respect the rights of persons, not even the vulnerable or families or persons on their land parcels. Like modern Israelis, unorthodox settlers may seize land from their rightful owners and manipulate the law to make these properties their own (Isa 5:8, 10:11).

The sin of these presumptuous self-aggrandizers is coveting (wanting and taking)—stealing and lying—whereby they hold Yahweh's Torah in contempt (Isa 5:24). Renewed Israel will live in a justified (straightened-out) Zion, with Jerusalem again laid right in accord with Torah (Isa 37:5).

To briefly summarize the structure of Bible prophesy in its convictions about human rights: In the presence of human injustice and violation—where family solidarity and inter-human covenantal unity is ruptured—nations are thrown into disarray and crisis.

The underlying injustice is rooted in violation of Decalogue standards: idolatry, murder, stealing, lying, coveting. The

Theology, Polity, and the Pacific Vision

underlying malaise leads to symptomatic violence and strife against peoples—especially neighbors. The pain of injustice then must work out its judgment, including harsh civil strife, natural disaster, and political distress.

The end of human injustice is not relentless and unending judgment but repentance to and forgiveness of the God of humanity, the restoration of community and the opportunity to begin anew, the restitution of shalom and of humanitarian peace or humanitarian rights, and blessedness follows this recovery of covenantal justice. Grace unmerited (Hosea/*hesed*) has the final word.

This secular appropriation of human rights doctrine of prophetic Hebrew ethics will now be worked out, with a case study on Rwanda to follow.

SIDEBAR ON PROPHECY: ABRAHAM HESCHEL

Abraham Joshua Heschel has shown a magnificent vision of *The Prophets* (1962). He shows the bearing of the ancient prophets in laying the foundation for the modern understanding of human rights. Prophecy, says Heschel, is not simply the application of timeless standards to particular human situations, but rather an interpretation of a particular moment in history, a divine understanding of a human situation. Prophesy is exegesis of existence from a divine perspective (xviii)

Here we see the crucial relevance of prophetic insight into the issue of human rights. Like prophecy, rights are an attempt to define the temporal against the ultimate, the artificial against the real, the transient against the lasting, the evil against the good.

Though similar to Greek idealism, which sets sacred ideas over against quasi-illusory perceptions and opinions, the prophets of Israel speak of what life was meant to be and must be within the justice of the one God of nature and history. Prophecy is therefore a charter of human fulfillment and ethical realization. Prophecy, says Heschel, is a way of thinking and a way of living (xviii). It seeks reconciliation of one to others, to self, to God, to right.

Ethics and the Wars of Insurgency

The prophets are troublingly concrete even trivial. Rather than grand themes of being, goodness, and truth, they speak of widows, orphans, plumb lines and yardsticks, corrupt judges and loaded scales. Crimes and misdemeanors are not just lapses or indiscretions; they are catastrophes on the world, demanding righteous indignation. For Heschel, injustice and wrong are injurious to people, death blows to existence, threats to the world (4) .That petty thievery, neglect of the poor, a tip of the hat to the queen of heaven, hypocrisy and falsehood would be cause for foreign invasion, the fall of Jerusalem, exile, and ultimately the destruction of the nation is incomprehensible to the conscience. It's just not fair.

As Joliet Jake in *The Blues Brothers* (1962) says to Elwood, who picks him up on release from prison in a sad replacement for the grand Cadillac, "You lied to me!" Elwood replies, "It wasn't lies, just bullshit." Prophecy for Heschel is "the voice that God has lent to the silent agony, a voice to the plundered poor against the profane riches of the world."[30]

God is concerned with the concrete situation, condition, plight and plea of every person. God is the guarantor and advocate (avenger) of human rights and all violations of such. So Job says, "I know that my avenger lives and at the last he shall stand upon the earth" (Job 19:25, paraphrase).

In the prophets' raged and uncomfortable rhetoric, God feels fiercely for people. Though rebellious and full of iniquity, humans are cherished by God.[31]

When the Jesuits or Belgian Reformed Protestants (who were killed en masse by the Spanish Catholics) came to Rwanda thy brought with them this doctrine of human worth. Regrettably, they also brought with them economic exploitation, educational and cultural hegemony, and brutal violence symbolized by amputated hands. Now the prophets and the human rights they bestow on the world live again. They are always contemporary.

30. Abraham Joshua Heschel, *The Prophets* (New York: Harper & Row, 1962), 5.
31. Ibid.

Theology, Polity, and the Pacific Vision

As a Rwanda killer is condemned in the dock at the Hague, we do not see only a scared and cruel young man who killed dozens, perhaps hundreds, near us in Srebrenica, but we witness a whole history and structure of evil, officers and teachers, politicians and priests, mothers, fathers, and village elders who failed to tell and do the truth. This is the same apparently, with the two children from Dagestan (Chechnya) who ignited the bombs at the Boston Marathon in 2013.

The prophets express the terrifying singularity and profound universality of ethical responsibility for Kingdom Israel. Now one who destroyed a single soul has destroyed the whole world and one who saves a single one has saved the whole world.[32] This mystical Kabbalism is normative prophetic Judaism, relevant to human rights doctrine but also overly sublime: like tiny Tim, "an octave too high for our ears."[33]

Yet despite its rigor, prophetic ethics alone has the power to bring human rights to the poor and powerless because of its conviction about the intervention of individuality and solidarity. Both the law and philosophy require universality and uniformity. Prophetic ethics embrace both individuality and solidarity. Prophetic ethics pertain to human rights in their specificity: the tyrant is condemned by the power of God (Isa 33:13); idols are shattered (Isa 2:18); war is strongly proscribed (Isa 8, Ps 20); a quiet habitation of justice will be established (Isa 11:10; 21:2–4); the messianic judge will be fair and good (Isa 11:1–9); God is the source of right (Deut 1:17); God establishes justice and will judge the earth (Gen 18:25; Isa 30:18). Righteousness (*tsedakah*) is the atmosphere and salience of justice (*mishpat*); if the underlying ethos is wrong, particular judgments will miss the mark.

32. Ibid., 14.
33. Ibid., 10.

111

Ethics and the Wars of Insurgency

EXCURSUS: HUMAN RIGHTS AND AN ETHIC OF PUNISHMENT

Two prophetic themes have a bearing on human rights: punishment and justice—and their correlation in forgiveness and mercy. Since this is a moral universe and persons are imbued with conscience, individuals and societies are held responsible for actions by God and through political orders. Found in earliest human experience, the theme of punishment (chastisement) gains sharp relief in the Hebrew prophets.

Scholars of prophecy find three purposes for punishment: retribution, deterrence, and reformation. By the time of the eighth-century prophets of Israel, deterrence and reformation had come to dominate a theology of punishment while retribution had began to recede as inhuman.

Practically speaking, retribution was self-defeating since it invariably set off another round of retaliation and violence and it simply did not work (Jer 5:3). Ethically speaking, humans began to see mercy, forgiveness, and restitution as nobler and more efficacious responses to human sinfulness and wrong.

Theologically speaking, as the nature of God came more into focus impressing that divine image more into human emulation and imprint on the personal and collective conscience, the divine will seemed to refine, repair, and renew the lives and life together of persons, communities, and nations.

The anthropology behind the prophetic (and pastoral) view of punishment is that humans are free in thought, will, and action. We are capable of being and doing good and evil. Sometimes persons and peoples decide for and persist in wrong. Such wrong inclination and wrongdoing either brings about censure, repentance, and new resolve to do right or it hardens into chronic and belligerent malice (Isa 63:17).

In the modern idiom we might say with Robert Jay Lifton that we are dealing with the psychopathological process of "doubling" (*The Nazi Doctors*, 2000), where malevolence and misdeeds are rationalized to the point where someone or some organization

Theology, Polity, and the Pacific Vision

loses conscience to the point where we torture or kill without the slightest qualms.

Punishment for the Hebrew prophets is physical, natural, metaphysical, and soulful. You don't have to be placed in stocks or in prison for punishment to be present and sorely felt. We experience punishment (Latin: *poena*; Sanskrit: *pu*, meaning pain and purification) in our tortured conscience and in the way the world, especially the social world, turns against us. The distraught uncle of the Boston Marathon bombers cries out against his own flesh and blood as "losers"—deserving of punishment. In a recent rash of child murders in my neighborhood, one father on my street said that his own son, who wildly struck out and killed an innocent boy, "deserved what he was going to get." Though we may seek to hide and remain unnoticed and undetected in anonymity, the prophetic vision, the God gaze, tells us that "our sins will find us out" (Num 32:23).

"Agony," writes Heschel," "is the final test." But what good is that? A poor older white couple in South Carolina this week pleas on the witness stand, "God knows we didn't do it." The charge: torture of a ten-year-old black neighbor boy. Our modern ethic, stripped of eschatological and ethical consciousness—of God, says blithely, "It ain't wrong if you don't get caught." Human justice only loosely coincides with divine justice. Humanly provided and protected rights can only faintly resembles those sacred endowments.

The ethical theory of punishment becomes the basis of penal theory. This in turn undergirds the legal apparatus of punishment. Human punishment is colored by locality and only recently universality. An American youth in Singapore is accused of defacing a sign and a sexual indiscretion of selling a marijuana cigarette. He receives the harsh punishment of imprisonment and lashings. Americans complain of the harsh injustice of this law. We especially abhor any forms of *sharia*.

Today we attempt to standardize human rights law: laws of the seas, laws governing warfare, prisoner treatment, etc.. When President Milosovich suspends freedom of assembly and press in Beograd, the world protests.

Ethics and the Wars of Insurgency

The human structures and processes of punishment and rights are messy at best. They tend toward understatement and overkill. Last night, after a lull for over one year, a terrorist bomb ripped through a Paris train station. Amid and after the grief for the dead and injured is a resolve to punish the bombers from President Chirac. Rights will be set aside, many innocents will be harassed and arrested, especially Algerians and Muslims. The planners and perpetrators may be isolated and prosecuted—probably not. As Gilbert and Sullivan quipped, "The punishment fits the crime."

More often, in terms of prophetic justice, those broadly responsible will go unpunished—especially the movers and shakers. Poor accomplices will be nailed and scapegoats will be hauled into the dock.

Before we move from prophetic to pragmatic factors in human rights, we must consider a vexing theological question that has bearing on the ethical nature of human rights. We can put it in the context of Michael Perry's work. If human rights in his thought are ineliminably religious—i.e., they require and assume the background of God for their power and efficacy—is religious fidelity a concomitant to human fidelity? If this is the case can there be sanction, law, rights, or punishment for irreligion or heresy? Is persecution for religion a crime under law?

Let us come at the issue from another angle. If Perry is right and the most rudimentary human law contains religious premises and presuppositions—e.g., the sanctions against blasphemy and idolatry—can persons be punished for committing those violations or can the prosecution of those offenses be prohibited. Can a secular government prosecute persons for religious hate crimes or is the matter simply beyond the reach of the law? If persons or nations violate the human freedoms and rights of "free exercise of religion"—worship and evangelism—are those abrogations reviewable in a world court?

The history is troubling. This is especially true in contemporary world society, where many if not most societies and nations are intensely religious, even verging on theocracy: America and

Theology, Polity, and the Pacific Vision

nominally Christian Europe and Russia, Israel, and Muslim nations ranging from secular-pluralistic states (Turkey, Indonesia) to full-blown *sharia* states (Pakistan, Iran, etc.).

In ancient Israel her pagan and polytheistic neighbors were punished by God and state for not only for inhumanity and immorality but for impiety and unchastity. Christians often killed and otherwise punished not only Muslims and Jews for false faith but pagans (South Amerindians) for their disbelief. My general belief is that this age is gone forever. Religious crimes are unprosecutable since theological knowledge is opaque and refracted. Perception of God's will and way is difficult to discern and verify and impossible to prosecute without causing moral offense. Still there is an inescapable religious dimension to human rights.

The first case is already enshrined and codified in human rights doctrine and legislation. The freedom to religious belief and expression is universally affirmed as a quintessential human right. China's suppression of the Dali Lama and the Buddhist nation of Tibet and America's disdain for Muslims—refusing them property rights for a mosque—are patent violations of those fundamental human rights. Israel has often taken its rabbinic law as a pretext to mistreat Arab Islam—and even Palestinian Christianity. Russia has subtly and officially mistreated Protestant sects, Muslim neighbors, and Jewish zealots and Zionists. She now officially persecutes and even executes Chechnyan Muslims on her southwest border.

Should such violations be officially docketed at the Hague? What of North Korea's persecution of religious zealots, including Christians? What of South Korea's sanctions against atheists and humanists? One sees the perplexity of such approaches.

The second case may have more currency in our world filled with so many religious and irreligious tyrants. If a "godless regime"—Mugabe in Africa, Verwoerd in South Africa, Pol Pot in Cambodia, Hitler in Germany, or Stalin in Russia, or one might even add Assad in Syria—turns against its own peoples and the world, committing blatant blasphemy, idolatry, injustice, and murder, should it be opposed and overturned on religious grounds alone—what Hitler's opponents, including Bonhoeffer, called a matter of doctrine and confession itself—*status confessionis*?

I would think so, despite quietistic views of the Pauline dictum that even treacherous states such as the Roman Empire are established by God, demanding our obedience (Rom 12). The intertwining of God laws and inter-human laws is so intricate that sins against God invariably lead to violence among people.

Theological respect and piety are therefore becoming for nations—even secular-humanist ones, even though these values cannot be prescribed or enforced. Honoring the God of all nations and faiths and displaying public piety is incumbent on any regime that seeks to do good and honor God. The delicate balance of faith and religious neutrality issuing both civic peace and spiritual integrity has been achieved in many modern societies including Switzerland, French Alsace, Canada, and the US. Refined religion, even Christian faith as a non-religious phenomenon (Karl Barth), is skeptical of itself. All religion, including Christian faith, is in part a human construction, and therefore always under the judgment of the first three commandments, proscribing atheism, idolatry, and blasphemy. Gentle estimation of one's own and generous respect for the faiths of others are marks of true faith and virtuous civility.

THE ECONOMICAL/POLITICAL DIMENSION OF HUMAN RIGHTS

I now must conclude this background analytical study and round out a further series of very brief and, of necessity, cursory, illustrative case studies—finishing Somalia and proceeding through Rwanda, Bosnia, 9/11, Iraq, Afghanistan, Pakistan, Iran, and Syria. I have written in another format of the Arab Spring and the crisis with Libya, in the autobiographical volume *While I Have Being* (2012).This concludes a near thirty-year undertaking on the ethics (including theology) of American foreign policy in matters of war and peace.

The final theme of analysis we explore is that of politics including economics. When the final outcomes we seek are in the

Theology, Polity, and the Pacific Vision

realm of law, human rights, and ethics, the sociopolitical vector becomes critical.

When Leonard Bernstein conducted the Berlin Philharmonic celebrating the taking down of the Berlin Wall, he changed the words of Schiller's text in the grand conclusion of Beethoven's *Ninth Symphony* from "Freude, Freude" to "Freiheit, Freiheit." In the same way Johannes Brahms in *Ein Deutsches Requiem* uses a common, down-to-earth idiom to transmit sublime and sacred themes. Now we see that earthly rights and goods are inextricably woven with heavenly realities.

The contention of this essay is that human fulfillment and well-being is the concern of God for humanity and the world. Such well-being is involved with the material and economic well being of societies. Today we see some societies in the world flourishing (Mexico, India, etc.), some experiencing slow growth and improvement (US, Brazil, etc.), some experiencing some economic threats at present (Euro-zone, China), and others in desperate straights (Africa, the Middle East, etc.). These market appraisals fall back against the spiritual and ethical atmospheres of different cultures. In the wide world we are all more and more intertwined in interdependence. This is not only the imperative of ethics but in accord with vital self-interest.

The humanistic or often-called "liberal" (freedom-oriented) view of the human condition and prospect begins with a critique and rejection of the religious biases of previous centuries. A generation of publicly minded citizens who are fed up with endless religious wars and offended by religious trivialization of life now say "No more." People now demand pluralism and toleration rather than religious domination and privilege. This occurs both in Protestant and Catholic lands and it lays the foundations of a new secular-humanist culture and civil order.

Dissenting minorities get their way, disestablishing both Catholic and Protestant establishments. When dissenters come into the majority—as is the case in "Tea Party" America, 2012 and 2013—and crave a "religious state," they find it is gone and they can't get it back. Stackhouse puts it vividly: "While England burned

Ethics and the Wars of Insurgency

with the flames of contending lights [the Smithfield martyrs], while Calvinist parties were snuffed out in France or rekindled in Holland and New England, philosophers became skeptical."[34]

THOMAS HOBBES (1588-1679)

Reason, not religion, had to be the ground for human rights for the skeptical Enlightenment. The religious Enlightenment which would follow a century later (Edwards and Wesley) returned to a fervent Calvinist ardor. The earlier traditions were several within this more secular school of thought. Thomas Hobbes, a conservative protector of the establishment, despised the seditious Puritan ministers as he wrote at the end of the Cromwellian revolt in *The Leviathan*. He shared an even more radical view of the Calvinist doctrine of depravity and the fall, finding it infectious in personal and public life. Life was "nasty, brutish and short," which made it necessary that human motivations and actions be sublimated to the goods of the state. Only in an "absolute social contract" where anarchic human impulses and other impulses of freedom were channeled into the civic good was order made possible, creating a societal milieu where human rights were possible. "Concerted and cohesive social fabric" (fashioned in the sublimating of human wills) alone could "insure peace."

Human rights, for Hobbes, are socio-legal constructs having no transcending or "higher law" derivation. These covenants and contracts of life have their beauty and power in human assent grounded in reason and freedom. Human rights, claims this wise man who invented them, are civil rights conceived and implemented in citizen thought, will, and action. The genius of Hobbes was his clear vision and statement of the human social contract (with political authorities) which insured solidarity and peace. The danger of his construal is its Machiavellian or Thrasmachian character—an arbitrary and expedient force to maintain order.

---

34. Stackhouse, *Creeds, Society, and Human Rights*, 65.

Theology, Polity, and the Pacific Vision

Hobbesian rights theorists must ultimately admit that there is no check on malicious and harmful will.

JOHN LOCKE (1632-1704)

An even more decisive and formative determinant of modern human rights laws and customs comes from the work of John Locke. Coming from the regions of radical freedom and dissent in Somerset and southwest England, educated at Westminster and Christ Church, Oxford, he spent extensive years in France and Holland during the religio-political strife in England. He returned in 1689 after the succession of William and Mary. His thought is therefore steeped in Cartesian skepticism and after his father, who was a Puritan divine—in radical Calvinism. By nature and training an empiricist and experientialist (physician), like Hobbes he believed in radical human freedom, knowing that the mind could fashion perceptions and convictions into operative beliefs, including the time-honored rights of man. He believed in natural law as a guide of nature, mind, and God transposed into the good and obligatory. He sought to enhance pluralism and toleration within a viable and vital commonwealth with strong ties to both England and America.

The legacy of his thought is found in the founders of this nation. It suffuses the thought and happiness of the consciousness of the American people as they desired to reach the levels of divine will in their political action.

The British utilitarians would blend both Hobbesian and Lockean ideas into a way of understanding human rights that would correlate self-interest and altruism, immanental and transcendental horizons. Private rights pertain until they are in conflict with the common good.

As these crucial centuries unfold into modern history and are enriched by contacts with German, French, and American thought—Kant and Hegel, Montesquieu, Rousseau and Voltaire—a foundational tableau of human values comes to understand a new global understanding of human rights. Blended in a cauldron

Ethics and the Wars of Insurgency

of colonial and anti-colonial wars, the emergence of new nations and global consciousness, charters, constitutions, tribunals, negotiations, and laws of nations and seas develop. A potpourri of salient ideas, values, laws, and beliefs takes form which will change the convictional and ethical character of the world and a greater and greater portion of the earth's peoples.

Twentieth-century humanitarian documents—the constitutions of new nations from Vietnam to Ghana and Bosnia; law settlements such as Nuremberg, the Hague, and Strasbourg; the League and United Nations; trade, mutual protection treaties, and economic unions—all follow this tidal wave of human rights: freedom and responsibility.

CONCLUSION: RWANDA, A CASE STUDY

As half a million Hutu trekked home after two years in UN refugee camps in Zaire, Jonasi Ruziga, a Tutsi leader, watched carefully. He remembered clearly the faces of those militant Hutu who had killed his daughters two years earlier. That genocide of the minority though ruling tribe had taken some 800,000 to 1,000,000 lives. Hutus had ruled Rwanda for a few short decades after independence in 1962 after the successful Hutu revolution in 1959. In 1973, the Rwanda Patriotic Front, a militant Tutsi faction, took over the government again and elections in 1981 and brought a semblance of participatory government, though the Tutsi held on to their historical preeminence. In 1994, after elections brought about a shared government, Tutsi leaders shot down an airplane carrying Rwandan president Habyarimana and Birundi president Cyprien Ntaryamana. The killing and ambush of other leaders led to the Hutu massacre of late 1994.

Before the colonial period, Rwanda (French: Republique Rwandaise) had been a quasi-stable society where the indigenous aboriginal Twa pygmies (hunters and potters) were joined by the Hutu tribes (perhaps in the tenth century) and then the Nilotic Tutsi in the fourteenth century. Though the Tutsi were always a small minority (10 percent) they ruled by virtue of their position as

Theology, Polity, and the Pacific Vision

aristocratic landowners and cattle-raisers, as a Mwami (god-king) ruled a hierarchy of Tutsi chiefs and military captains. The tightly organized and administered civil system included a mechanism of taxation and military conscription.

The Hutu—mainly subsistence farmers and vassals—resisted this Tutsi-dominated governmental structure even though they constituted 90 percent of the population. Part of German East Africa in 1890 and the Belgian Congo in 1916, and extended in a mandate in 1923, she came under disruptive European colonial presence and conversion to the Roman Catholic faith. Today, after successful missions of the Belgian Reformed (Calvinist) Church (Pastor Vincent Van Gogh's communion), 15 percent of the present population is Protestant.

As Janasi Ruziga watched each returning pilgrim he held all of this history in his mind and gaze, along with a most remarkable spirit. "I saw two of the killers of my daughters—they passed along the road just like that—this morning I saw one more . . ." In the view of many Tutsi, had Ruziga seized a machete and hacked his children's killers to pieces, he would have been acting "within his rights." Yet he did not. "I will wait," he said, "until everybody has returned. Then I will go to the authorities and make my report." Perhaps his daughter's killers will join the some 800,000 present Hutu detainees standing in crowded jails awaiting prosecution.

Ruziga continued:

> . . . whatever happens will be up to the government. If they find that they killed because they were told by the authorities, then I will agree to live with them the way we lived before.[35]

Remarkable composure and sense of justice. Even the Nuremberg prosecutors did not accept "I was only following orders" or "They would have killed me if I refused" as excuses. The generals in the first tribunal and the doctors in the second used these words and they faced the gallows. The doctors were indeed worse than the generals as they developed policies of sterilization and forced

---

35. *Time*, December 2, 1996, 44–45.

Ethics and the Wars of Insurgency

abortion. They also invented for history "ktenology"—gruesome innovations in the "science of killing."

Was there some belief in crude justice or moral retribution in Ruziga's conscience, thinking that things would go his way in the Tutsi courts? Did he have some uncanny hope that human rights, justice, forgiveness, and killer confessions would make things right? Whatever—in the midst of an agonizing history, a new hope and vision came to life.

RWANDA AND GREATER AFRICA: A CASE STUDY

The eyes of the world have been riveted on western Zaire and eastern Rwanda as we in the Euro-American world celebrate the "bleak midwinter" of 1996. Our mind journeys to the Horn of Africa, even to Somalia, as we meditate on the star and magi (one African?) along with the precious parcels they bore—precious stones, gold, frankincense and myrrh—products of Mogadishu. We also celebrate the birth of a child who caravanned with his weary parents into Africa to escape Herod's infanticide.

As families trek back home in Rwanda only to face the cruel and capricious gunmen called the Rwanda government forces, they are not sure about what they will find or what they are about to face. The children—always the cruelest victims of starvation and war—cry out to us. Bereft of family, the ten-year-old carries his baby sister, who dies in his arms, and the heart of the onlooking world wrenches in agony. "Why? Good God—why?" "It is Jesus—the Son of God—our brother." We sell the needy for a pair of shoes (Amos 2:6).

Safety and sustenance is not forthcoming from the world's uneasy conscience and our wealth and largesse does not seem to translate into real prevention of hunger and healing of pain. The aid can't seem to get through on either side of the border. As soon as assistance arrives corruption gobbles it up. As always, the poor and sick, women, children, and elders seem to get the crumbs and leftovers. Political opportunists and warring tribal factions grab up any supplies before they get to those in need. Even though the

Theology, Polity, and the Pacific Vision

NGOs do awesome work, the thugs and governments insist that provisions go through them, which is where it ends up.

Peace-making and peace-keeping here will require stern admonition to those at once despicable and pitiable overgrown boys wielding swords. Perhaps we will have to require disarming these guys, which is like cutting off their identity. Even detention or more severe punishment may be required.

But this won't happen. The Western nations lack resolve based on the insidious doctrine "Let the Negras kill themselves." Twenty whites killed in Blackhawk Down and we hightail it out of there. Westerners say they lack resources and legal mandate—disguises of our indifference despite the documented fact that the white man's violating and emasculating colonialism caused this crisis in the first place.

A more serious and credible factor is that the human rights creed is in its infancy—just beginning to evolve. Foolish bickering (does African moral leadership belong to Anglophones or Francophones?) is rife. Political leadership across the board lacks the Nelson Mandela kind of ethical courage and statesmanship. No one will say that this whole terrible business is wrong and must stop. Everyone cites sheer overwhelming need as an excuse to stay home, pat the security of one's own wallet, and enjoy Christmas.

Meanwhile, the sublime irony. Jesse Norman sings on the stereo:

> I wonder as I wander out under the sky, why Jesus the savior did come for to die,
>
> For poor ornery creatures like you and like I, I wonder as I wander out under the sky.
>
> If Jesus had wanted for any mean thing, a star in the sky or a bird on the wing,
>
> Or all of God's angels in heaven for to sing, he surely could have it, for he was the king.[36]

America is now poised to celebrate Thanksgiving—now a ritualized indulgence—perhaps to satiate our jaded conscience

---

36. John Jacob Niles, "I Wonder as I Wander" (1934).

Ethics and the Wars of Insurgency

about pain we contribute to and refuse to help alleviate—shopping until we drop—beginning with Easter—then the mimesis of violence—football and basketball seasons—all a grand distraction from the liberating work God has for us to do in his creation.

The UN Security Council has declared a humanitarian mission to central Africa spearheaded by Canada but joined by America, Africa, Europe, and other nations. As America prepares to extend its Bosnia peace-keeping efforts for another year, this extra call up is opposed by isolationists and moral cynics. We must see that we need to bring a two-pronged beneficence to the world—"To whom much is given . . ." The world needs to continue formulating its doctrine of humanitarian human rights, its creed of compassion, and so realize the preconditions of that kingdom of rights.

The African crisis now (1996) threatens five countries in addition to Somalia. In an update to this book I will add an addendum (2013) that will deal with current crises derivative of the history traced here—including Syria, Iraq, Iran, Pakistan, even a note about Korea and China. At present (mid-1990s) attention has been focused on Zaire, Birundi, Uganda, Rwanda, and Congo. The mission has been to stop fratricide and lawlessness long enough to heal the sick, feed the hungry, clothe the naked, and shelter the homeless—the classical biblical and interfaith imperative which we have identified as the prophetic imperative.

How did the helplessness and homelessness come about? This is the question after the domestic and international sin that is the etiology of this crisis and the key to its solution. We must ask: Where did the Hutu militia in the Zaire refugee camps get their weapons? How was the minority government of the Tutsis endorsed and put in place? What will be the further bitter fruits still to come of Belgian colonialism before justice has run its course? What will be the historical consequences of the broader wrong of Euro-American exploitation that has plagued the region from the nineteenth century through the Cold War and into the present events?

Theology, Polity, and the Pacific Vision

Let us now position the regional crisis of American foreign policy and global ethics represented by the word Rwanda. A film—*Hotel Rwanda*—and a trail of sequelae that continue to perplex the conscience. In Rwanda these are the only stigmata of the genocide lingering two decades later—except for a modestly successful economy within a desperate continent and a historical miracle called the truth commissions and forgiveness rituals.

How can we theologically evaluate the events we have reviewed in the light of prophetic history? Reaching such a perspective considers: (1) assigning the requirements of righteousness, (2) acknowledging the calculus of sin and calamity and the failure of public justice, (3) declaring the requirements of guilt, complicity, and honest confession and reparations, and finally (4) laying out the conditions and processes of reconciliation and hope. In biblical ethics, moral regression and calamity are linked—as are justice and hope. Prosperity and new beginnings in hope are the fruits of righteousness. Consider the panorama of biblical prophesy as it pertains to national and international events—to theological and political realms of life:

1. Moses links Torah obedience with success in the new land.
2. Samuel claims that God's will and God's Way alone command supreme loyalty.
3. Nathan condemns the hedonistic and militaristic propensities of King David.
4. Amos condemns the political idolatry of Israel as it gives occasion for human contempt.
5. Hosea speaks of the enduring faithfulness of Yahweh even in face of our faithlessness.
6. Isaiah envisions return and restoration when the warfare (price of justice) is accomplished.

The structure of moral reality given in the Hebrew prophetic tradition mandates humanity to put in place systems and processes of human rights to offset the ever-present human danger of economic exploitation, political ambition, and aggrandizement

Ethics and the Wars of Insurgency

and militaristic aggression. Only in this way can we offer havens of justice and peace amid prevailing human injustice and warring madness.

EXCURSUS: SOMALIA IN MINNEAPOLIS, WINTER 2013

Back in Africa—Maiduguri to be precise—the murdered bodies of Muslims (some say Islamists) are being hauled in and dumped at morgues in north Nigeria—hopefully not baptized with the urine of contempt as at Abu Ghraib.

Meanwhile, back in the US heartland—in Minneapolis—the food fight started in South High, an infamous simmering ghetto of the inner city. The provocation? The same crime—ethnicity, faith, shame, hatred. Whites and African-Americans, yes, but another forceful community throws the spaghetti: Somalis and Somali-Americans. With the fierce pride we know well from Mogadishu—they fight back against the double-barreled assault—as we used to say of the same coalition in south Chicago, "Black and white together, arm and arm together, against the poor." At last discrimination is being challenged and happily the weapons are mashed potatoes. And Hubert Humphrey and Frits Mondale look on with pity.

In conclusion of this Rwanda section, we set the stage for the discussion of a perplexing Syria, which now culminates the two-decade turmoil that the US and the world have experienced since Somalia.

First, we must ask the question, what primal righteousness (*shalom*) has been violated in these agonies in the Horn of Africa? The thesis I have proposed holds that humanitarian crises are matters of ethics, and even theology, not simply "security," "national interests," "expedience," and "political aggrandizement."

Of course the objection is raised, "We can't bail out every troubled nation on earth." I grant that the US cannot rescue and support with "social work" the billions of distressed peoples in the world. When eighteen army rangers were killed in one skirmish

Theology, Polity, and the Pacific Vision

with a tribal gang in Mogadishu, many Americans decided that African lives—even hundreds of thousands—were not worth a single American life. As in Israel with reference to Palestinian lives, this twisted ideology is sub-ethical and unworthy of the God of all humanity, for whom all persons are precious and of infinite value.

Hutus and Tutsis have lived at peace and equilibrium for centuries. Both tribes have a sort of affinity for the other—perhaps a begrudging reciprocity that they need each other. Both have come under the spell of missionary Christianity—Roman Catholicism for the most part. The trans-border crisis began after Hutu thugs crossed the border, went on a rampage, and killed over one million of the Tutsi minority, though the ruling Tutsi minority constitute only 20 percent of the population. Now, with countless other Tutu that have fled Rwanda in search of security from revenge in Zaire, those rightly accused of mass slaughter are also making their way back home.

The war crimes tribunal set up after the 1994 genocide, in the view of some commentators, constitutes part of the problem. A general witch-hunt for those who instigated, executed, or failed to resist the genocide would implicate almost every living Hutu. Something like forgiveness or amnesty is required. Hopefully this would come after sincere contrition and restitution on the part of the perpetuators.

As in Germany, made known in the telling scholarship of professor Goldhagen at Harvard, nothing can be done now among a generation of seventy-to-eighty-year-olds, all of whom were either actively involved in or looked on willingly in silent complicity with the Shoah. Most joined in, cooperated, or at least knew and remained silent. Only the grace offered through the ministries of Judaism—the religion of the victims—can cleanse the lands of Germany, France, Poland, Austria, and others who were "Hitler's willing executioners." Only repentance and new resolve into the terrifying train of sequelae such as we are pondering can help the world at last find some semblance of peace, closure, and new beginnings.

Ethics and the Wars of Insurgency

After the Rwandan atrocity, eighty thousand Hutus were convicted and held in Tutsi prison camps—with no hope of fair trials, the conclusion of justice, or new starts. We must continue to press for specific justice for the guilty in these cases. We must also reconnoiter with the broader and deeper history of colonial violence that Belgium, France, England, Italy, Holland, and the US inflicted upon Africa. Otherwise the lethal legacy will continue to bear its bitter fruit—the fruit of the lynching tree and amputated hands. Today those nations involved can extend reparative help along with the ministries of churches and NGOs to breathe new life and humanity into this abused and mistreated sector of the world. Present-day Belgians like my daughter and granddaughter can never today recompense for the gross brutality of King Leopold and the all-to-willing Belgian people of a century ago. We can and must revisit those lands with ministries of kindness, admonition, and upbuilding.

INTERLUDE: FROM RWANDA (1996) TO SYRIA (2013)

My line of reflection is about global affairs in their theological and ethical aspects. This has been my bona fides for fifty years—political, economic, and biomedical ethics. I began the war-and-peace work—global politics—with the book on the Gulf War (1992) which preceded this previously unpublished work on Somalia and Rwanda. This resurrected, hand-produced piece was compounded with notes of further conflicts in the years 1993–1996 which I now culminate in provisional reflections on Syria (2013).

After that initial work I turned to the earth-shaking and nation-challenging crisis of 9/11. Here the books *Ethics and the War on Terrorism* (2002), *Jew, Christian, Muslim: Faithful Unification or Fateful Trifurcation?* (2003), and *Journey into an Interfaith World: Jews, Christians, and Muslims in a World Come of Age* (2010) were published. During the 2007–2013 period I wrote *America in God's World: Theology, Ethics, and the Crises of Bases Abroad, Bad Money, and Black Gold* (2009) and two autobiographies that deal

Theology, Polity, and the Pacific Vision

with issues such as Iraq, Afghanistan, Iran, Palestine, and Pakistan through the Bush Jr. years and the beginnings of the Obama presidency. These were also published by Wipf and Stock—*While I Have Being* (2011), which included material on the Arab Spring, and *For Such a Time as This* (2013), which deals with the difficulties of Obama's first term and the difficult frustrations of the beginning second term (through 2013) when he was confronted by a recalcitrant congress and regressive political movements such as the ill-named "Tea Party." Now, as if this were not a full enough plate, along comes Syria even while we are trying to quit Iraq and Afghanistan.

This present book now concludes with what might become the new "Permanent War" (G.W. Bush after Kant's " Perpetual Peace")—the unfolding quandary in Syria.

There seems to be no quick and permanent solution (*deus ex machina*) at hand. All signs point to an intricate, long-developing and therefore irremediable situation. It has to do with Israel/Palestine, Lebanon, Iraq, Afghanistan, Iran, with implications running out even to Russia, China, and North Korea. It also bears on the nascent, yet inconclusive, events of the Arab Spring (2011).

If it is dangerous to write on in-process history, how much more dangerous it is to not write on something that may be unending and deeply harmful to human good. One of my teachers, Paul Lehmann, after his teachers Reinhold and Richard Niebuhr, said that the marching orders for an ethicist first ask the question, "What now is God doing in the world?" This is the question that we must address to the situation in Syria, for she has become the epicenter of the seismic changes now going on in the world.

EXCURSUS: SYRIA

I close this book with a brief and tentative excursus on "wars of insurgency" in our theologically turmoiled time. In an interview with Charlie Rose (May 5, 2013) at the time of his landmark article in *The New Yorker* (May 13, 2013), Dexter Filkens sketched an outline of the new—yet wearily old—situation in Syria.

Ethics and the Wars of Insurgency

Here are the features of the present situation: With seventy thousand killed in three-plus years, a new report is received on chemical weapons attacks on civilians near Damascus. This was one of the great cities of the ancient world where two millennia ago one Saul of Tarsus, a synagogue heresy interrogator, became the Apostle Paul when he was thrown from his horse on one of the ancient Roman roads.

This event changed world history, transfiguring secular history to become the history of Emmanuel—the God of the Messiah/Word/Logos. Nature now decisively became Creation and history became Holy History. Today in Taurat, along the Mediterranean coast of Syria just north of the Lebanon border, the women and children have been massacred and burned to death. Government soldiers have insisted that civilians proclaim President Assad—God. The blasphemy and contempt of justice, even divinity—the reason for the collapse of the old Roman Empire—is still with us.

And the "blue haze gas" that appeared in rocket blasts—killing and choking animals and humans—was either sarin or mustard nerve agents. They seemed to portend the very disintegration of this revered biblical land.

Even with Israel's bombing of certain weapons stores in Damascus—seemingly arriving in daily flights from Tehran to Damascus—there was no evidence of a corridor of transmission into the hands of Israel's arch-enemy Hezbollah in Lebanon. Granted, Hezbollah, was an essential component of the government's brutal kabal sustained by daily Russian flights of ordinance to Damascus.

We may never know since the US and Israel—one the greatest power in the world and the other the earth-sovereign in the Middle East—act with impunity quite removed from the normal ethical conventions of war. Like the days before the Jewish, Jesus, and Paul revolution of Spirit (God and good), evil and godlessness has again triumphed.

Filkens continues his diagnosis and recommendations:

America should provide shoulder weapons—"man-pads"—to selected "safe rebels" in order that they might shoot down government-fired Scud missiles and take out some government

Theology, Polity, and the Pacific Vision

air defenses—the next best thing to an Americo-Euro-Israeli imposed no-fly zone. Yet again history proves that "those who have the power and the gold make the rules"—Stokeley Charmichael's "Golden Rule."

Troops on the ground should not be used—this should be a bloodless, no-sacrifice-required, drone-executed battle, preferably carried out by Turks or African mercenaries.

Syria is reputed to have the largest "active" chemical weapons in the world.

Possible end scenarios (extricating ourselves) might include: (1) an Allowaite enclave on the seacoast—perhaps the old Saul/Paul region, (2) a Kurd nation patched together from these homeless wanderers from the several contiguous nations, (3) a permanent civil war where Sunni and Shiah struggle incessantly till one or the other is eliminated—as if the Issac/Ishmael fratricide ever could be resolved.

Perhaps it would end in the creation of another Lebanon where again ancient lands of beauty and glory become permanent seedbeds for strife. (4) Quite probably we might be in store for a messy fifty or one hundred years as massive conflict ensues between the Shiah axis—Iran, Syria, Lebanon, etc.—at odds with a Sunni axis—Saudi Arabia, Egypt, Iraq, etc. As elsewhere, Sufi will provide martyrs for both jihadist schools of Islam.

American fundamentalist militants will continue their Islamophobic and Zionist manias—secretly harboring apocalyptic dreams of a world free of Ishmael, gays, socialists, and other pacifists. Meanwhile John McCain—a most complicated militant, actually a student of Reinhold Niebuhr (see my *For Such a Time as This*)—calls for arming the rebels and imposing a no-fly zone along with other air assets while he yearns to be rid of the messy Middle East and be back in the more simply Manichean orbit of the Far East and Vietnam.

The geopolitical and theological ramifications of the Filken's articles follow Tom Friedman's wisdom on the Middle East in dispatches to the *New York Times* and books in the train of *From Beirut to Jerusalem*. Bewildering chicanery, ambiguity, and

Ethics and the Wars of Insurgency

indecisiveness (political sins of commission and omission) is profuse from Ben Ghazi to Damascus. All nations deserve reproach—America, Israel, Britain, Europe—for their widespread mendacity and deceit (Rashid Khalidi), bloodthirsty violence excused as faith in the Islamic world, and, to top it all, lethal inaction—in Russia, China and most of the rest of the world.

The loose, lost, and scattered weapons—mostly made in Russia, China, and the US—have been released into this volatile region—inevitably to come back to kill and maim (e.g., land mines and assault weapons) the children of those who manufactured them. Cold war and hot war simmers on unabated.

Beyond the seventy thousand Syrians now treacherously wandering as war refugees, there are the near four million homeless refugees—the biblical widows and orphans—whom it is ethically our bonded duty to save and succor. Genocide, herbicide, deicide, fratricide, and patricide (the killing of countries) is rife and there is "no health in us" (*Book of Common Prayer*).

This constellation of events and consequences of unfortunate decisions is the inevitable result of ill-chosen decisions in the Middle East, especially in Israel and Palestine. The Boston brother bombers from Chechnya put it differently. "The US—our homeland—went to kill Muslims in Iraq and Afghanistan—killing one of our own is killing all of us."[37]

Our well-and-good, indeed imperative, decision to guarantee the survival of Israel by condoning her belligerence against Palestine has made this conflict the exacerbating infection at the center of illness in the global body politic—especially inciting the global war on terrorism.

The cognate interventions of the US—the invasions and occupations of Iraq and Afghanistan, disputes on Iran and Syria, movements toward drone and espionage warfare—all radiate from this underlying malaise of Israel/Palestine. With this chain of events the world has squandered manifold resources and inclined the world away from life-building and towards violence, bloodshed, and the stunting of lives. All high religion says with Jewish

---

37. Author's paraphrase from new reports.

Theology, Polity, and the Pacific Vision

Kabal that to save one human being is to save the whole human race—the kill one is to kill all. The brothers in Boston miss the point.

Religion, regrettably, has been part of the problem and not the answer. In the cascade of events we have traced faith has been an active force in the malaise of our times. Since 1993 in Somalia and 1995 in Srebinica—when Serbian priests blessed the marching holy warriors as they killed seven thousand Bosnian Muslims—religion has been turned from the will of God toward evil. The contemplated actions of Jewish Israel, Christian America, and jihadist Muslim regimes holds the world hostage to such malevolent and unholy purposes. In our composite iniquity we have turned the world away from the truth and disgraced the holy laws of the God of Abraham.

Often ambitions and actions have begun with good intentions—providing a safe homeland for the near-exterminated global Jewish diaspora, ridding the world of the profoundly evil Osama Bin Laden, freeing Iraq from the tyrant Saddam Hussein, reversing our earlier course of supporting tyrants who terrorized their own peoples, and encouraging the arousals of the Arab Spring toward freedom and democracy. All these were good deeds but not unalloyed—tainted as they were with self-aggrandizement and exploitation of the weak on the earth, proving the old dictum that "The road to hell is paved with good intentions."

MAY 23-24, 2013: OBAMA RESETS AMERICAN POLICY ON WAR AND PEACE

Our national ethics of war and peace may be an example of such misguided good intents. President Obama made the first major policy statement of his second term in two installments. In an open press conference he handled well and gracefully a protester who wanted to go on record in opposition to GITMO. She felt that the hunger strike of over one hundred Yemeni nationals now found to be innocents should be honored—they should not be force-fed but released and allowed to return home. In a second

Ethics and the Wars of Insurgency

event at a military academy, the President's talk set out a redirection of American foreign policy.

1. The redirected policies appear as follows: Constitutional, legal, and ethical principles should lead us to continue to secure the homeland as well as possible (i.e., continue our massive global anti-insurgency network) and sustain specific anti-terrorist tactics, including drones, targeted killings, and the "collateral damage"—a euphemism for the numerous innocent children in Pakistan killed by our bombings. At the same time we will need to diminish this imprecision and the illegality/immorality of detention of innocents, torture, Abu Ghraib, and like breaches of human dignity. Rather, we should honor the freedom and dignity of all persons—even so-called enemies and suspected terrorists.

It now remains for the world to salvage and enhance global interfaith cooperation as we build the earth toward justice and peace. We need to let the world recover from fratricidal religious and nationalistic hatred, abuse of the earth, and economic distortion harming the poor and vulnerable wretched of the earth. We need again to shepherd this "Good Earth" toward becoming the realm of God wherein all lives and all peoples are blessed as the "stars of the sky and the sands of the seas."

2. We went to war after 9/11, leading the whole earth into what we wrongly believed was a cosmic Manichean conflict of good and evil, the godly against the godless—America, Israel, and allies against the Islamic world. It was overkill, to say the slightest, leading to a decade of global strife of which Syria is the latest theater. In fact the global Shiah axis—Afghanistan, Iran, Hezbollah and Syria—may be poising itself to a suicidal fight to the last man, as proved to be the case of the furtive British incursion into the Khyber Pass in the Afghan War of 1838–1841.

3. The War on Terrorism, convened by the new axis of Britain/America to invade Iraq on false pretenses—that it was responsible for 9/11 and in possession of weapons of

Theology, Polity, and the Pacific Vision

mass-destruction—was followed with the disgrace of torture, GITMO, Abu Grahib, etc., and even at this early moment in the aftermath it is believed to be a fatal mistake—even on this Memorial Day when we sing "The Battle Hymn of the Republic"—"I can read His righteous sentence by the dim and flaring lamps—His day is marching on."

4. Now we must make our "marching on" more discriminating, precise, and free from deadly "collateral damage," which has a way of becoming of far greater magnitude than the enemies killed.

5. We will now consult Congress more fully as we transfer the direction of the War on Terror to the Pentagon from the CIA. We will continue our scheduled withdrawal from Afghanistan and Iraq and perhaps even reassess our one-sided support of Israel against the martyr people of Palestine, whom we all now in our secret hearts believe constitute the real cause of the War on Terrorism.

6. Our value approach in a foreign policy of war and peace must become "smart" and "proportional" ("just war") so that we restore support and ethical credibility on the home front and abroad.

7. We feel that we must retain a massive security infrastructure in the world and thereby "dismantle any specific networks of terrorists" (those who want to kill as many of us as possible) even if this expenditure threatens the fiscal well-being of our nation and world—poverty, healthcare, wellness of children and youth as well as elders.

8. "Why do they hate us?" we ask in disbelief. The suicide bombers in Boston from Chechnya and the Nigerian killers of a British military band drummer say they are responding to our prior actions which have been hateful, imperialistic, and wrongfully violent toward others. We have killed Muslims in Iraq and Palestine—so they are partially right and partially wrong. We often labor under the illusion that we are God's solely "chosen people," the greatest power in the world,

and that we should therefore have the power to "dominate the world." After all, didn't God tell us to "subdue" and "have dominion" over the world (Gen 1:28)? At least we feel that we are called to help defend the "American way" of freedom and democracy—our sacred heritage. These are all partially valid national beliefs and values and partially out of keeping with those same values.

Tony Candelaria and her closest friend and neighbor, classmate Emily Conatzer—both nine—were found in a hallway in Plaza Towers Elementary School locked in a loving embrace, now in death. As the dark, whirling tornado ripped through the school they clung to each other—reminding us of the old song of Patty Page—"Cling to me, speak my name, for we have only each other in this precipitous night." Together we trust that they found they found light and love and life. Only this love can overcome fear and death. This is the message that the President brings to the town and families of Moore on this Memorial Day/Trinity Sunday.

Today some partisans say they seek to bring the "will of Allah" to the earth while in actuality they disgrace the very name of the One God of Israel, Jesus, and Ishmael. We have chosen to live in our own self-deification in the face of the reality of God and the good he has set before the world.

Christians contend on earth for its peace, which first rose in the stars over Bethlehem, to where the magi came from out of Iran, Somalia, and Syria. Yet today Nigerian Christians attack Muslims in the north with machetes and haul their murdered corpses into the hospitals and morgues of the land. Meanwhile Israel—now a nation among the United Nations—seeks to secure *shalom* and radiate well-being into all the peoples of the world. And one Ben Adam, Ben Joseph—the one come for all the earth—sits across on the precipice west of Zion and weeps for the city, knowing the peace that is there for the taking and making—if only we would.

Kenneth Vaux
Evanston, Illinois
Summer 2013

Addendum
American Led Attack on Syria? (September 2013)

I FIRST ADD a synopsis on human rights from a colleague at Cambridge University.

MATRIX OF HUMAN RIGHTS[1]

Horizontal Axis (Defining Human Rights):
1. Social Rights—Family life, privacy, recreation/leisure, education, choice of partner, lifestyle, sexuality, housing
2. Economic Rights—Basic living standard, earn a living, work, social security, savings, choice of spending
3. Civil/Political Rights—Free speech, vote, fair trial, stand for office, join organizations, join union, strike
4. Cultural Rights—Cultural expression, cultural practices, clothing, religious expression, intellectual property, land rights
5. Environmental Rights—Pollution free, poison free, wilderness, beauty, sustainability, access to land

---

1. Adapted from James Ife, "Human Rights from Below: Achieving Rights through Community Development," lecture material, Cambridge University, 2009.

Addendum: American Led Attack on Syria? (September 2013)

6. Spiritual Rights—Choice, religious expression, rituals, experience nature, personal fulfillment, sacred land/objects
7. Survival Rights—Life, food, water, shelter, clothing, health, safety

Vertical Axis (Discussion Criteria Relating to Each Type of Rights):

1. Cultural, religious, philosophical and ideological transitions and understandings of rights—There are different constructions of human rights from different world views, shaped by culture, philosophy, religion and ideology.
2. Individual and collective understanding of rights—Human rights can be understood both as individual rights (the rights of an individual person) and as collective rights (the rights of a group).
3. Rights in the private/domestic and public/civil domain—Human rights apply not only in the public sphere but also in the domestic sphere, e.g. the right to freedom of expression in civil society and the right to freedom of expression in a family.
4. Rights and protection through courts and legislation, justiciability, etc.—To what extent are these rights justiciable (i.e. guaranteed or realized through legal processes: laws, courts, legal action, prosecutions, etc.)?
5. Rights and oppression: class, gender, race, age, disability, sexuality—Human rights violations are more frequent and more serious among oppressed or disadvantaged populations.
6. Responsibilities: individual, family, professional, community, civil society, state, world—All rights imply responsibilities, and the realization and protection of human rights make no sense if the corresponding responsibilities are not specified and enacted.
7. Intergenerational responsibilities to past and future generations—The responsibilities that go with human rights do not only exist in the present. We acknowledge responsibilities for

Addendum: American Led Attack on Syria? (September 2013)

human rights violations in the past, and a responsibility to future generations.

8. Education, facilitating dialogue, consciousness-raising, community awareness, action—Human rights will only be realized if people are aware of them, and of their role in constructing, claiming, protecting and facilitating the rights both of themselves and of others.

The drama unfolds with a pain and poignancy that this nation has seldom experienced. Yes it has happened before. Germany unleashed mustard gas in the trenches of WWI. America used nuclear weapons in the WWII and Iraq's use of gas against Iran is infamous. Wilfred Owen's WWI poem rightly attributes the atrocity to the depths of depravity and cruelty. His words become the anguished cry of the Akedah Offertorio on Benjamin Britten's *War Requiem*.

> *Tenor and Baritone: Peter Pears as the British soldier, and Dietrich Fischer-Dieskau as the German. They shriek in octave interval then modulate into a serene unison lament.*

So Abram rose, and clave the wood, and went,
And took the fire with him, and a knife.
And as they sojourned both of them together,
Isaac the first-born spake and said, My Father,
Behold the preparations, fire and iron,
But where the lamb for this burnt-offering?
Then Abram bound the youth with belts and straps,
And builded parapets and trenched there,
And streched forth the knife to slay his son.
When lo! and angel called him out of heaven,
Saying, Lay not thy hand upon the lad,
Neither do anything to him. Behold,
A ram, caught in a thicket by its horns;
Offer the Ram of Pride instead of him.
But the old man would not so, but slew his son,
And half the seed of Europe, one by one.[2]

---

2. Wilfred Owen, "Parable of the Old Men and the Young" (1918).

Addendum: American Led Attack on Syria? (September 2013)

Médecins sans Frontières (Doctors without Borders) first reported the gruesome atrocity, which had come in several installments. In the most recent release of "gas" in Adra, near Damascus, youth were struck blind like the zealous persecutor Saul of Tarsus—perhaps on the same old Roman road. One thousand were killed—including over four hundred children. The horror of persons gasping for breath—the grim pictures of crying babies clinging to their lifeless moms and crying moms clinging to their lifeless children—horrified the world, until after a few days some—any some—tried to do something—anything—about it.

Eventually the "war-wearied West" and others who had grown accustomed to unspeakable violence—considering the poor, old, sick, wounded, and dying as discomfiting flies to be swatted away—turned on the TV and lit another cigarette. With two million displaced and one hundred thousand already killed, these irritable disgraces of displaced and threatened humanity now seemed to be just another bad late-night movie.

The only thing that seems to move us is the love of the rich for more and the powerful for greater domination. Conventions of "just war," commandments against murder? Brush the floating dust under the carpet.

The evidence among the ashes and dust is incontrovertible say MSF and UN inspectors. "Yeah, like WMDs in Iraq," sighs a cynical world. "We can't get bogged down again on foreign soil."

KERRY IN GENEVA

Then, as scenes of 9/11 were rehearsed against the blue searchlights of the New York skyscape—an unexpected turn. President Bashar al-Assad of Syria has agreed to turn over his vast stockpiles of chemical weapons to the UN for their destruction. Russia had brokered the deal to spare his ravaged nation from the further disgrace and degradation of an American missile attack.

How had this state of affairs come about?

Some background: As I showed throughout this book, our present crises are the outcomes of a long war history—WWI and

Addendum: American Led Attack on Syria? (September 2013)

II, Hitler and Stalin and their crimes against humanity and genocidal war crimes, and more recently the sequence of events from Somalia to Syria, including Iraq's gassing of civilians in the Iraq/Iran war.

In a way—in a theological and moral sense—events also follow moments in American war history. "All have sinned and fallen short . . ." Our use of WMDs (nuclear bombs) against Japanese cities and the more remote and diffuse crimes against humanity in the extermination of the American Indians (in part from biological [germ] warfare) and the "Great Passage"—which W. E. B. Du Bois claimed took one hundred million lives—have brought this indictment on ourselves.

The American Civil War—Lincoln's divine judgment against the sin of slavery—saw brother killing brother, neighbor killing neighbor—reenacting the primal universal human crime of Cain and Abel—and of Jesus' admonition after Leviticus—"Love your neighbor as yourself." We do the very things we know we ought not and we refuse to do what we know full well is our duty.

Our conflicts today are not our mythical electronic "War Games," our hero figures, or some new "Cowboys and Indians" contention with good guys in white prevailing as they ride into the sunset with the "red men" dead in the dust. It is not ninja figures fighting against grotesque machines or animals or frightening zombie concoctions.

The propensity of construing war in Manichean terms—"othering" the enemy in some grotesque caricature, while we the God-chosen exceptionals express our "Manifest Destiny"—does not work in Syria, as it did not work in Iraq or Afghanistan. It is not easy here to so anathematize others since enemies now are neighbors, co-religionists, and friends. In the words of the famous cartoon, "We have met the enemy and it is us."[3]

Germany in WWI and Iraq in the 1980s used chemical weapons even in the face of the conventions binding the community of nations. Israel as well as Syria has not admitted to having WMDs which the whole world knows they have. America now

3. Walt Kelly, *Pogo*, August 1970.

Addendum: American Led Attack on Syria? (September 2013)

feels an obligation as the "most mighty nation in the world" to be the guardian of these hard-earned "norms" of global ethics. The UN Security Council seems immobilized by the threatened veto of Russia and China—the former an ally of Iraq with geopolitical issues of conflict with America, the latter with convictions of honoring the sovereignty of all nation-states. In America, liberal, international-law-oriented persons like Obama, Kerry, Hegel, and Ms. Clinton feel the moral imperative to stop such illegal and unethical action—even though it requires taking highly unpopular action.

Richard Lugar, the former senator of Indiana and Rhodes Scholar, feels that we should not bomb since our vital security interests are not at stake. Prof Ian Hurd, our own Northwestern political science professor, is deeply steeped in the high obligation imposed by international law, and believes that Syria has violated this law and that America would also be in violation if we bombed because we are not being attacked as a nation. MIT professor Noam Chomsky holds that American action would only be justified by a UN resolution. His student, my son, a professor at Cambridge, finds any and all killing reprehensible. Retaliation simply compounds the evil as more innocents die.

CHARLIE ROSE INTERVIEW WITH BASHAR AL-AASSAD[4]

Assad: We do not believe the US—remember Iraq? We have to expect the worst from the US—her record is clear: intervention, attack. and occupation. The Middle East is an interlocked region. Any attack will cause repercussions—direct and indirect. We are under contracts with Iran, Russia, and Hezbollah. They are our partners as Turkey, Saudi Arabia, and Europe are your partners. As Israel does not say if it has WMDs, we do not say if we have them. On August 21, 2013 peoples

---

4. What follows is my paraphrasing from the interview, broadcast September 9, 2013, on PBS.

Addendum: American Led Attack on Syria? (September 2013)

were attacked with chemical weapons—these included our own soldiers. "The terrorists did it." Israel and the US are opposed to bans on WMDs. You remember that Colin Powell, VP Chaney, PM Blair and others gave the world false information. What we have are allegations, not facts. If it happened I would have known about it and approved it. My plan is to stop the terrorists and cut off their outside support, then we can have an internal referendum and bring together all the parties in the country. The Al-Qaeda terrorists use religion for their purposes. We are a secular state bringing people together of all faiths. We have public support—therefore we fight on. Tunisia, Egypt, and Libya have no public support—the Arab Spring failed.

Rose: Your father, whom I know and have interviewed, fought against the Egyptian brotherhood and killed them all.

Assad: When you fight the enemy you must kill them all. You must exterminate them. The gangrene must be cut out.

President Obama's response: When dictators perform atrocities they watch to see if they get away with it. Violations of international law are also dangers to our homeland security. Weapons will spill out and endanger allies like Turkey, Jordan, and Israel. I'm president of the world's oldest constitutional democracy. Tonight I send Senator Kerry to Geneva. We've got to hold the line.

As October breaks, warm gusts still waft from the cooler ground. The gracious president of Iran charms the UN and Syria—and Syria, with Russia's prompting, agrees to dismantle her chemical weapon stockpiles. Both plead with the US and Israel to back off of our own belligerent reliance on WMDs.

It is homecoming at Northwestern. A side report reveals that US Navy Seals have attacked Somalia and "taken out" suspected "terrorists." The searing memory of *Blackhawk Down* still burns and they still hate us—and we wonder why.

Addendum: American Led Attack on Syria? (September 2013)

A PAINFUL REVERSAL

At the end of 2013 the crisis in Syria and indeed the global theater of the "War on Terrorism" made a painful reversal. Although my central operative thesis—that the Israeli occupation of Palestine, following on the heels of pushing out of the land millions of Arab Muslims and even Christians, was the cause of the "War on Terrorism"—was still maintained, now the heroic portrayal of the opposition in Syria also started to fray. The opposition had become "Islamist"—even Al Qaeda—in ideology, and the US—its staunchest supporter—was now the enemy.

On the Iranian front, an astounding gesture by the new president to dismantle the development of any sort of WMDs and nuclear weapons and submit to full oversight and inspections was forthcoming. Israel was skeptical and persisted in her perceived right to strike Iran if she felt threatened. She also held the US hostage to her views and the media did not dare to challenge her in her conviction that she deserved immunity from critique. Just as it was not kosher for the media to report Nelson Mandela's condemnation of the state of Israel's policies and programs against the Palestinians ("Our freedom is incomplete without the freedom of the Palestinians"), even the progressive media, e.g., MSNBC, could not forward critiques of Israel's persistent belligerence even to the point of being willing to destroy the American and Allied peace process with Iran.

As fragile Christmas peace settled in a now de-Christianized East Jerusalem and Bethlehem, the "War on Terrorism"—both the insurgency and counter-insurgency—brought on night, which seemed dark as night could be, with no shepherds or other politicos singing with the angels, "Peace on earth, good will to all."

> The summer is over. The harvest is gathered in—winter is here and we are not saved." (Jer 8:20 paraphrase)

As summer transpires into autumn the world wonders what harvest we have planted. Hope is there, as is the gnawing doubt and fear. But we must go on—hoping against hope.

www.ingramcontent.com/pod-product-compliance
Lightning Source LLC
Chambersburg PA
CBHW051107160426
43193CB00010B/1352